HOK London

HOK
London
Diversity in design

Kenneth Powell

Foreword by Sir Peter Cook

Laurence King Publishing

Foreword by Sir Peter Cook

Ken Powell sums up so well the very particular way in which the London office of HOK makes its own very particular trajectory: one that gives reference to its origins as a firm, yet must exist within a dense architectural milieu. It is as a ship making its own way down a busy sea-lane, in touch with the rest of the fleet but negotiating tricky tides and waters. Skilful piloting and a well-balanced crew are essential.

The pilot has surely been Larry Malcic, who has gained the confidence of the British by, in certain senses, becoming very much like them: sensing the ebbs and flows as much as charting them. Dealing with the wide mixture of cultures and talents on board. Encouraging both the confident and the shy amongst his crew with equal respect.

Yet in three years as an 'insider/outsider' to the office, I have observed an unexpectedly valuable contingent of architects who really understand the culture of buildings – their fabric and nuances – and then respond in the most sensitive ways: calmly and without a mawkish over-valuation of the second-rate just because it is old. As a conspicuous 'futurist' it may seem odd that I single out the conservation element of HOK for special praise. Watching it at work, listening to its processes as it sets forth on an analysis of a building, a remnant or a site and developing a strategy of replacement, I find myself once again delighted to be in the role of a student of architecture.

London is a deceptive city: though apparently intact, it is far from homogeneous and it has flourished through an almost impossible collage of interventions and oddly interpreted dreams. Rarely are any of these sustained for more than half a block, and some of the best architectural ideas occur behind the façade, in the courtyard or round the back somewhere. At best, that same ingenuity and application of nuance can be applied to new building, so looking through this book I commend to you the careful corner, the charmed recess, the tucking and folding of surface, the accumulation of planes.

In those same three years there have been intriguing changes to the architectural community of London and to the ways in which it can apply itself to its task. The HOK office reflects this: no longer an Anglo-American set-up, any team may be made up of architects from every continent, educated in any of a hundred universities. Yet the Pole and the Malaysian, the Yorkshireman and the Sikh lady will probably have been to the same lectures and be referring to the same details. London architecture is part of world architecture. The computer homogenizes, the approaches to the tasks are hybrid and are then subjected to the regular occasions upon which Jan Pietrzak and I join Larry for the reviews. Not every office in London would submit to such interference, but not every office in London has such thoroughness either.

The relationship of the work to the waves of fashion and public utterance is a subtle one. I am not sure that the office would really relish making an 'icon' building, for such things usually emanate from a bloody-minded position that deliberately bypasses the world of nuance and assimilation. Similarly, I am intrigued by its relationship to 'High Tech' – which has been the most successful British mannerism in recent years. The detailing that it has generated has become, effectively, part of our vernacular, with HOK's take on it best seen in the Darwin Centre at the Natural History Museum. It is a rich and dense technology that parallels the intrigue with working parts and the lacework of surface that inspired the High Victorian context of South Kensington, in which this new piece finds itself.

Forty Grosvenor Place is another instance of technical architecture being enjoyed: particularly in the contained territory. HOK's work is often at pains not to jar the behaviour of the street and much time and discussion lies behind the circumspection of its architecture. Pushing this all forward is the very active transportation group who get in there amongst state-of-the-art working parts and gizmos that surreptitiously affect our attitude towards fabric and the new vocabulary of architecture. Parametric formulation and the soft territory between digital drawing, digital assessment of criteria and simulation all parallel the new vocabulary with a new methodology.

Finally, one can observe that the new, young, multicultural crew bring an intriguing cross-current of influence into our English tradition of good behaviour at the front and fun and games at the back, and I observe that Malcic is also intrigued by this and well able to absorb the challenge.

Contents

Introduction

Opposite The Enlightenment Gallery within the magnificently restored King's Library at the British Museum.

HOK and London

HOK International is a formidable presence on the landscape of architectural practice in London in the first decade of the twenty-first century, but its London office is just one of 26 branches located across the world, employing in total over 2,500 staff. Beginning in London with interior design work, the practice has expanded to offer diverse design services. The sheer range of the practice's work in London – from new-build offices at Canary Wharf to restoration, refurbishment and interiors work on virtually every government building in Whitehall; the reconstruction of two of the capital's largest hospitals; an extension to the Natural History Museum; and even a church in leafy Dulwich, one of the few built in London in recent decades – reflects the degree to which HOK has become rooted in one of the most dynamic cities in Europe. The idea that HOK is solely an 'American' practice is palpably absurd. From London, the firm works on projects across Europe and the Middle East; its staff are internationally recruited. Yet there is something reassuring about the location of its offices, a surprisingly calm haven above the throngs of shoppers on Oxford Street. This design studio in the heart of the West End is a microcosm of London; staff from 30 countries speaking many languages mirror London's status as a cosmopolitan world city. But HOK, no matter where the relevant office or project is located, values its roots, and, like every respectable institution, its founders.

History

HOK was established in St Louis, Missouri, at the very heart of the United States, in 1955, with a staff of around 30 people. Amongst the founding fathers of the firm, the name of George Hellmuth is pre-eminent. Born in St Louis in 1907, the son of a prominent local architect, and educated at the city's Washington University, Hellmuth worked for a time for the practice of Smith, Hinchman & Grylls in Detroit. Hellmuth had the idea that a good architectural practice should be a troika, with one of the three partners responsible for administration and marketing, a second running the design side of the operation and the third getting the buildings built. Accordingly, he formed the partnership of Hellmuth, Yamasaki & Leinweber in 1949. Joseph Leinweber was to be the firm's financial manager; Minoru Yamasaki, the designer, was subsequently to gain fame as the architect of New York's World Trade Center. The practice, with offices in Detroit and St Louis, lasted only six years. However, the partnership Hellmuth then established in 1955, back in St Louis, with Gyo Obata and George Kassabaum – both of them associates in his former practice, and some years younger than himself – was to prove more durable. Hellmuth chaired the board of HOK until his 'retirement' in 1971, but then assumed the chairmanship of HOK International. He died in 1999, having acquired an additional reputation as an expert ceramicist in his old age.

Hellmuth was essentially the visionary genius who built the practice into an international force. Gyo Obata – born in San Francisco in 1923 and trained at Berkeley, Washington University and at Cranbrook under Eero Saarinen – was an outstanding designer who had worked for a time for Skidmore, Owings & Merrill's (SOM's) Chicago office. The last survivor of the founding triumvirate, Obata is recognized as a major figure in American architecture. His expressive use of concrete in two works of the early 1960s, the St Louis Planetarium and the centrally-planned chapel for the Benedictine community in the suburbs of that city, attracted international interest. Obata's inspiration underpinned subsequent major projects, including the Houston Galleria (North America's first enclosed retail mall), Dallas/Fort Worth Airport and the National Air and Space Museum in Washington, DC. The extraordinary temple for the Reorganized Church of Jesus Christ of Latter Day Saints in Independence, Missouri, completed in 1993, is one of his most striking later works. Obata has declared that 'listening to the client's needs' has been one of HOK's great strengths. In this way, he argued, 'HOK is able to understand the variables of a project and to use the potential of those variables in arriving at the appropriate design solution.'

George Kassabaum (d. 1982) was the partner who oversaw the construction of projects, a man legendary for his approach to controlling costs. The practice took off quickly, with school projects initially dominant and most of its work concentrated in the Midwest. Within a few decades, however, HOK was an international name. George Hellmuth had, in fact, developed a formula for a successful practice, which he implemented at HOK. Diversity of work, both in terms of building types and locations, was vital, he argued. The firm should also develop specialities such as landscape design, interiors and urban planning. Finally, good administration was imperative: the firm should be efficiently managed and properly marketed. This formula obviously worked, since by

1982 HOK had nine offices and around 800 staff.

Larry Malcic, today HOK's design director in London, recalls all three founders: 'Each was very different from the others, but all three were uniquely talented in complementary ways.' Malcic had studied at the University of Pennsylvania, attracted there by the formidable reputation of one of its leading teachers, Louis Kahn. Kahn, says Malcic, 'was a huge influence, as was (Sir) Peter Shepheard'. British-born Shepheard, dean of the school at Penn for most of the 1970s, was a highly respected landscape designer as well as architect. 'He was a great urbanist, with a holistic, truly humanist vision of design', says Malcic.

HOK in London
In 1989, Malcic was asked to join HOK, come to London 'for a few years' and establish what was initially a relatively small office. Other large US practices, notably Skidmore Owings & Merrill and Kohn Pedersen Fox (KPF), were

also working in London at the time. They had been attracted largely by the prospect of work generated by the 'Big Bang' of 1986, whereby financial markets were deregulated and international banks flooded into London, demanding huge dealing-floor spaces of the sort created at Canary Wharf and Broadgate in the City of London. North American experience of 'fast track' construction was particularly prized by British developers charged with meeting the demand for such spaces.

HOK's first London office was in High Holborn, and the goal from the start was to create a broad project base in line with the ideas of Hellmuth. The decentralized managerial structure of HOK (a private company in which no shareholder owns more than 10 per cent of the shares, and whose equity is owned by its employees) gave freedom to shape the London operation specifically for Europe, and not as merely a branch of the American practice. HOK was keen to develop a

range of specialities and skills in the London office, including, for example, interiors, planning and landscape design. A transportation group was soon formed under the direction of Richard Spencer – HOK has since worked with Rogers Stirk Harbour + Partners (formerly Richard Rogers Partnership) on the Terminal 5 project at Heathrow airport (where HOK is also the architect for the rail facilities). 'I wanted us to be a practice with values and vision,' Malcic says, 'generating new ideas, developing projects with clients that exemplified our commitment to improving the environment by conserving great work from the past and creating elegant and sustainable examples for the future'. A prime task was acquiring local knowledge to balance HOK's vast range of expertise acquired on projects internationally.

Working with Context
HOK's first big project in Britain was not, in fact, in London but in Glasgow, where it worked (designing retail interiors) with GMW and Reiach & Hall on the St Enoch shopping centre,

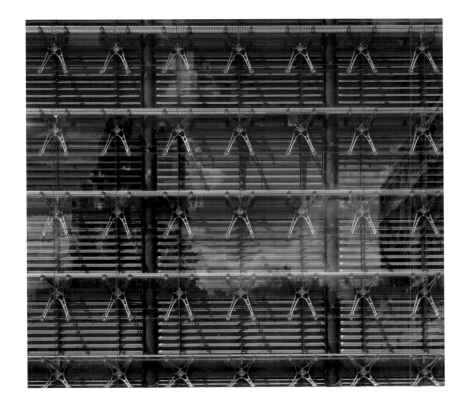

on the site of a demolished Victorian railway terminus. Its first important London job was the refashioning of the listed Britannic House (see pages 26–31), a major building by Edwin Lutyens in Finsbury Circus, as the world headquarters of British Petroleum, whose predecessor (The Anglo-Iranian Oil Company) had commissioned the original building in the 1920s and which was now moving back into it. HOK had designed BP America's offices in the USA, but the Britannic House project was not one it would have encountered across the Atlantic. The building was listed (Grade II*) – indeed, it had been listed as long ago as 1950. Both the City planners and English Heritage monitored every aspect of the scheme, on which HOK worked with the principal project architect Inskip & Jenkins. Much of the internal space – radically transformed by the insertion of a new atrium – consisted of fairly routine offices, but there were spaces – the boardroom and entrance lobby, for instance – which retained significant Lutyens details. The project had to

reinforce the sense of heritage in the building while equipping it as a modern headquarters for a global corporation. It involved, on the one hand, the insertion of modern services and, on the other, the design of new marble floors as part of the replanning of routes through the building. It was a matter of 'building on history', with new work which did not replicate the past but worked with it with a sense of continuity. The new fit-out, says Malcic, is 'neither uncompromisingly contemporary nor traditional, rather something which, because of the quality of both the design and the materials used, will last well'. That statement sums up some key elements of HOK's work in London over the subsequent decade.

Entering a competition for a new church in the London suburbs was not a move that might have been expected from a thrusting international practice making its mark in Britain. However, Malcic was determined to win the commission for the new St Barnabas, Dulwich, after the Victorian church on the site burned

down late in 1992 (see pages 40–9). In the event, HOK secured the job in the face of competition from several practices with extensive experience of church design. With its 20-metre (65-foot) high glass spire, designed in collaboration with engineer Mark Whitby, and rich stained glass by artist Caroline Swash, this is a building with a strong historical resonance but no explicit references to history – a further indicator of the flavour of HOK's forthcoming work in London. The project may not have been financially profitable but it probably changed perceptions of HOK in Britain, suggesting that the firm was here to stay. It certainly changed Larry Malcic's life, since he met and married a member of the congregation and, to this day, he is treated as a member of the church family whenever he visits St Barnabas.

Working with context seems to come naturally to HOK, so the competition for a new office building at Grosvenor Place on the edge of Belgravia was one that the practice was determined to

win. It beat some big names in British architecture – Hopkins, MacCormac, Farrell – to win the commission for Forty Grosvenor Place, another of the projects that convinced observers that HOK was 'here to stay' (see pages 76–85). The exterior of the building is, like St Barnabas, a reflection of HOK's search for a practical modern vernacular that respects history and tradition but eschews literal historicism – it has the solid, rational dignity of the best Classical architecture, without the 'trimmings', but with a significant emphasis on sustainability.

Conservation and Public Work

The repair, restoration and refurbishment of historic buildings – many of them Grade I listed national monuments, such as the Palace of Westminster (see pages 164–7) and the British Museum (see pages 124–9) – has become something of an HOK speciality. It was probably no coincidence that the practice's move into a broad range of public work came in the early 1990s, when the commercial development scene was hit by recession. The negotiated merger in 1995 with the well-established London practice of Cecil Denny Highton, with that firm's staff joining HOK, was a foundation of this process, since CDH had worked extensively on government buildings since its foundation in 1960. The merger saw HOK's office grow: staff numbers tripled in two years. It led to the move in 1999 to Oxford Street, where a large area of the Peter Robinson store was secured and refurbished to the practice's own designs (see pages 68–73). It now provides working accommodation for over 200 people. As a consequence of the merger, John Denny of CDH became a director of HOK, leading work for the government sector and being succeeded in that role in 2001 by Andrew Barraclough, who had led the project management group at CDH. Barraclough has organized and directed some of HOK's largest projects, including the redevelopment of the Ministry of Defence (see pages 140–51) and the ongoing reconstruction

of St Bartholomew's and the Royal London hospitals. Another recruit in 1995 was David King, whose skill and attention to detail was recognized when he was chosen as technical director for the merged organization.

Marlborough House, a Crown property adjacent to St James's Palace, was the first pre-nineteenth-century building that HOK's new conservation team had worked on (see pages 32–5). The Commonwealth Secretariat, which occupied the house, wanted to greatly improve the office accommodation there, update services and facilities and to restore the historic fabric. The project allowed for an element of inspirational new design to be woven into the historic complex, without compromising its cherished character. Neil Cooke's work on extending the Cabinet War Rooms in Whitehall and creating space for the new Churchill Museum is equally straightforward – at least superficially, although the project was technically extremely complex (see pages 168–73). As

a result of these projects, Cooke, who heads the practice's extensive conservation group, claims that there is not a basement in the whole length of Whitehall which he has not explored.

HOK's work in Whitehall, under the guidance of Andrew Barraclough, reflects central government's move to learn from the private sector, use its buildings more efficiently and provide better working conditions for the staff for whose services it must compete with the commercial sector. The Ministry of Defence (MoD) building, a huge complex designed by Emmanuel Vincent Harris before the First World War but completed as late as 1960, was badly equipped for the team working that the MoD wanted to implement, with warrens of cellular offices along corridors and dire staff facilities. Reconstructing the building – HOK was part of a successful Private Finance Initiative (PFI) bid with contractor Skanska – took five years, cost more than £350 million and involved decanting around 3,000 civil

servants and service personnel (see pages 120–3). Offices are now almost entirely open-plan. Formerly used for storage, its ground-floor pillared hall is now the social focus of the building – its café a place where staff meet informally. The bronze standard lamps, designed in the manner of Harris, are a nice touch, reflecting the architects' skill at stretching the budget to include elements of delight. A restaurant spills out into what was a gloomy lightwell, and is now a glazed atrium. There is a modern conference suite, and – though the details cannot be disclosed – the building has been made far more secure at a time when terrorism is a real threat to those working for the government. Discussing the way in which the MoD was subtly updated, Ray Lane of HOK, who worked on the project throughout, insists that 'we have no house style: we do what is appropriate'. Larry Malcic adds: 'HOK doesn't indulge in meaningless gestures and irrational form-making for its own sake. Clarity, coherence and consistency are key features of our

work. A sense of order and legibility in a building reassures those who work in it or visit it and emphasizes the elements of surprise and distinction.'

New-build Design

Whether in the context of existing historic structures or new-build work, HOK certainly warms to a highly practical brief. One such was that for the Darwin Centre at the Natural History Museum, another milestone project for the London office (see pages 110–19). HOK's rationalism fits easily alongside Alfred Waterhouse's great museum building – itself a highly ordered, rational modern structure beneath its veneer of historicism.

HOK is a practice that does not often repeat itself, and which is, at times, intensely self-critical. The recruitment of Sir Peter Cook, renowned pedagogue and ex-partner in visionary 1960s group Archigram, as a design principal at HOK places him in the role of regular critic. Though he has been heavily preoccupied with work on

HOK Sport's 2012 Olympics projects, Cook is a frequent visitor to the Oxford Street offices, debating with the team, involving himself in competition projects and providing an illuminating overview of the work. Only an open-minded practice would consider an appointment of this kind.

A glance at any HOK project will usually show evidence of a desire to break the mould and reject the formulaic. Working at Canary Wharf, in a landscape of buildings by Cesar Pelli, Foster & Partners, SOM, KPF and other international practices, HOK managed to do exactly that in its 93,000 square metre (1 million square foot), 32-storey headquarters building for Barclays Bank (see pages 130–9). Building at Canary Wharf means working with formulae – the central core tower is standard practice. HOK managed to quietly subvert the established model by offsetting the cores, creating larger floorplates and providing a series of atria, which bring natural light into the building and act

as social and interactive space for the 6,000 staff working in the tower. The Barclays building is classic HOK, wearing its innovations lightly. Its move to Canary Wharf, from a number of buildings in the City of London, was linked to a culture change at Barclays, which generated the focus on interactive space. The lightness and clarity of the new building is not compromised by the lashings of marble and granite typically found in the lobbies of buildings at Canary Wharf – the reception area here has a cool and elegant austerity that expresses efficiency and a sense of purpose in business rather than the need for extraneous display. Canary Wharf has not in the past been noted for its progressive stance on environmental issues, yet the Barclays building achieved an 'excellent' rating from BREEAM (the UK's Building Research Establishment's Environmental Assessment Method) for its low-energy servicing strategy. It is certainly the only tall building in the area so far to boast a 'green' roof,

and Barclays has not been slow to publicize its contribution to reducing carbon emissions. Above all, Barclays is a highly practical building, made for intensive use.

Just across the dock from Barclays, HOK's tower at West India Quay is equally innovative, combining 12 floors of hotel space – probably the boldest move yet by the Marriott group into contemporary design – with 160 apartments on top (see pages 152–7). The building sits next to the West India Dock warehouses, the most important surviving group of eighteenth-century dock buildings in London, its brick-clad podium providing a contextual 'footstool' to the sheer glazed tower above. The latter has a deliberate relationship with Pelli's nearby One Canada Square tower, rather than with the weighty, masonry-clad Postmodernist blocks around it. It is also, incidentally, the tallest post-tensioned structure in Britain. London's Docklands is home to many residential developments that are merely run-of-

Opposite SJ Berwin's 'Stanley's' staff restaurant provides a dramatic contrast to the more formal work environment.

Right Restored committee room at the Palace of Westminster.

the-mill, but this one is set apart not just by the boldness of its concept but equally by the refinement of its details – the sculptural mailboxes in the lobby to the apartments, for example, provide an enjoyable touch of fancy. They could have been simply attached to a wall, but HOK decided there was a more interesting way to address the issue.

The element of continuity in HOK's philosophy of design – stretching back to the early days of Hellmuth, Obata and Kassabaum's practice in St Louis – remains strong. Obata, though a hugely respected designer, always resisted the temptation to create 'signature' buildings or to cultivate a house style – each commission had to be approached individually, and the needs of each client assessed with no preconceptions as to how they should be addressed. The stress on teamwork and diversity was also there from the start. George Hellmuth was 'convinced that any individual who depends only on himself puts a definite ceiling on his potential accomplishments,' adding,

'however, if he is willing to work with the best men he can find and has enough skill to identify these best men, there can be absolutely no limit to his professional achievements.' The teamwork ethos is very much alive today. Perhaps it helps that HOK has no 'big signature fronting its operations; there is a reassuring continuity in the initials. And the emphasis on efficient delivery of projects is a theme that runs through everything the practice does. In London, David King and Andrew Barraclough oversee this key aspect of its work.

Interiors
HOK has plenty of high-profile jobs, but equally important ones rarely seen by the general public – the many office fit-outs, for example, a number of them for prestigious law firms, which tend to be very demanding clients with the highest expectations. These are substantial projects: SJ Berwin's headquarters in the City houses around 1,000 staff (see pages160–3). Reynolds Porter Chamberlain, with around half

that number, occupies a Richard Rogers building next to Tower Bridge but went to HOK for its office fit-out (see pages 150–1). Interiors projects of this sort are immensely demanding, but the results are often seen only by regular users. They also require an understanding of the culture and habits of those users. Aileen Asher, HOK's director of interiors, has made this knowledge the focus of her career. She is the consummate interpreter of the workplace needs of corporate and professional clients. You could hardly conceive of a more tradition-minded, even 'establishment', body than the All England Lawn Tennis Association. Its clubhouse at Wimbledon, the ultimate shrine of the sport, was refashioned by HOK with a 'traditional but contemporary touch', which respects those traditions but also allows for change (see pages 106–9). It is the approach that has been successful in the practice's governmental work, where an equal element of tact is often needed. In many cases, the very success of the project lies in

its near-invisibility. Working on the committee rooms at the Palace of Westminster, for example, was a slow process, since the rooms were only empty when Parliament was in recess – it took a decade to refurbish 20 rooms (see pages 164–7). Every aspect of the services – ventilation, audio systems, security and lighting – had to be upgraded, but the historic fabric had to remain unchanged. Worn-out leather seat covers were replaced like-for-like and hand-blocked wallpapers applied to the walls after the original AWN Pugin patterns. As Neil Cooke admits, many of the MPs returning to the refurbished rooms probably hardly noticed that any work had been done: that was the mark of the HOK team's success.

The Wider Context
HOK's London office also works, of course, on projects far beyond London. Telford College in Edinburgh is only one example of HOK's work outside London. The Netherlands is an important market for the firm: HOK's

Dexia Tower is the tallest building in central Amsterdam, where the practice was also responsible for the passenger terminal in the eastern docks. Retail centres designed by HOK stretch from Portugal and Spain to Kazakhstan, with prominent new developments underway in Ljubljana, Slovenia and Zagreb, Croatia. In the Middle East, the firm is building a 45-storey headquarters for the Central Bank of Kuwait and is extending Jørn Utzon's Kuwaiti Parliament building. The transportation group led by Richard Spencer opened the new Cork, Ireland airport in 2007 and is now designing new terminals for Bahrain and Delhi. Relationships with clients surmount frontiers, as demonstrated by Aileen Asher's activities in the corporate workplace. Corporate clients call on HOK's design strength to deliver workplace and interior design solutions across the capitals of Europe. Working with ExxonMobil on American projects led to a commission to fit out 17,000 square metres (180,000 square feet) of offices in London for the company

(see pages 86–9). (HOK seems to have something of a monopoly when it comes to headquarters buildings for oil companies.) HOK works for ExxonMobil in Europe, Africa, the Middle East, and faraway Sakhalin Island, north of Japan.

The Future
London, however, remains home to the office, and much of its best work is happening in the city. The mix of public and commercial jobs that has stood the practice in such good stead since the early 1990s continues. There are major urban masterplans – for the West End of London and Canary Wharf, for example – and office projects such as Bow Bells House on Cheapside and the remodelling of the British Medical Association's headquarters in Bloomsbury. Securing, with Skanska, the PFI project to rebuild two of the big London teaching hospitals, the Royal London and St Bartholomew's, was a huge coup. The £1 billion-plus contract is scheduled for completion in 2014 and will

transform healthcare in east London. Historic buildings, some of them Grade I listed, are being incorporated into the two developments.

In many respects, HOK International's success in London seems to be the product of the practice's pragmatism, adaptability and passionate commitment to addressing a client's brief. But there is a vision beyond the practical achievement that involves inspiration, innovation and creativity. The formula of 'local knowledge plus global expertise' seems to be a sure one in a city where planning issues often involve vocal public debate but where few question that city's global role and the need for architecture that works in tune with it. Whether it is in Whitehall, Westminster, the City, Docklands or the suburbs, HOK's diversity of work seems in harmony with London because, like all the best London architecture of the past, it pays regard to history but addresses the needs and issues of the present age in order to ensure a sustainable future.

Site Locations

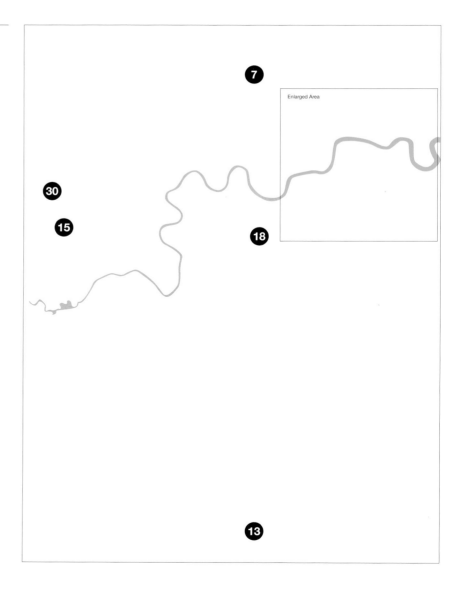

Projects

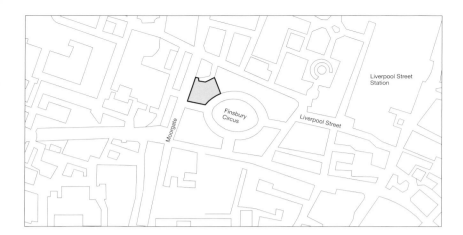

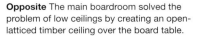

British Petroleum World Headquarters

Finsbury Circus, City of London
Client: British Petroleum
Completion: 1991

Context

The BP World Headquarters project was the first job in the UK capital to be undertaken by HOK's London office, launched in 1989–90. HOK's strong links with the oil industry in the USA, where it had worked for Standard Oil (which was acquired by BP), were instrumental in its winning the commission. However, it was far removed from the practice's previous projects in this sector of business.

BP's London headquarters had long been housed in Britannic House, a 1960s tower adjacent to the Barbican Centre – it was later comprehensively refurbished and re-clad as City Point. The older Britannic House in Finsbury Circus, which had been built as the headquarters of the Anglo-Iranian Oil Company – predecessor of BP – to designs by Sir Edwin Lutyens in the 1920s, had previously been let by BP, which now decided to reoccupy this outstanding building. (Lutyens' biographer, Christopher Hussey, described Britannic House as 'a raging

beauty, decked, though with a new look, in all the armoury of classical opera'.) The building, of Portland stone on a steel frame, had been listed as early as 1950.

Brief

HOK's brief from developer Greycoat was to work with the practice of Inskip & Jenkins, which was in overall charge of the restoration project. The scheme included the creation of a new, central, glazed atrium as part of a strategy for re-equipping the vintage landmark for modern office use by around 450 employees. A number of interiors, including the entrance hall, main stair, chairman's office and boardroom, were to be retained much as found – along with surviving Lutyens furnishings. Other spaces, including a multiplicity of dining rooms and kitchens, were seen as irrelevant to late twentieth-century working practices. Both English Heritage and the City planners took a close interest in the scheme. The transformation was, however, in many respects

radical. BP wanted a minimal amount of cellular office space; throughout the building, the emphasis was to be on flexibility and team working, with outdated spatial hierarchies jettisoned. As is so often the case, the move to a new building coincided with a searching re-examination of the company's operational culture and management structure in the context of its global strategy.

Solution

The plan of the building, as completed by Lutyens, was complex and apparently inseparable from the compartmented character of the spaces within it. Opening up the interior meant creating new routes, with nodes where they connected acting as directional markers. Inlaid wood and marble were used at these points, as 'compass roses' in the manner of Lutyens, to define the new routes. The layout of the internal office spaces was developed by HOK in close consultation with the future users, who were able to select their preferred

Left Restored entrance hall complete with steel plate floor salvaged from an oil tanker.

Below The café area provides a modern interpretation of Lutyen's original window fenestration.

Opposite Inlaid floors, with 12 different kinds of marble, act as directional markers for routes within the building.

workstation layout using elements from a standard furnishing system. (Under the 'new order', virtually every member of staff had an equal area of office space – private offices were very few, though directors were allowed to specify their own bespoke furniture.)

The aim was to reinforce the existing character of the building wherever possible. There had to be a strong sense of continuity, though there was no attempt to create pseudo-Lutyens decor. The look, HOK believed, should be neither pedantically traditionalist nor incongruously contemporary, but should have classic elegance and durability. The relatively generous budget, allowing for the use of high-quality materials, certainly helped the architects to achieve this aspiration. Using computers and the HOK Draw drafting system to develop the complex floor patterns was an innovative move, presaging the application of new technology to work in historical contexts. The result is work of a quality that compares well with that done in the 1920s.

The architects in HOK's new London office were hugely impressed by Lutyens' work, and learnt a great deal from the BP project. The Edwardian architect's loadbearing stone façades were highly efficient in environmental terms, such that the energy consumption of Britannic House was notably lower than that of BP's 1960s tower. HOK put these lessons to work in its designs for a new office building at Grosvenor Place (see pages 76–85), while the successful strategy of creating new working areas in a period building was further developed in their Ministry of Defence project (see pages 140–9). Britannic House was, however, significant in its own right as a project where the enhancement of a historic building was combined with a thoroughgoing shake-up of an organization's working practices, demanding a highly innovative spatial strategy.

Opposite Contemporary timber and glass screen viewed through a Lutyens doorway.

Right Vestibule to the executive offices.

Far right A typical executive office.

0   10   50m

Fourth Floor Plan

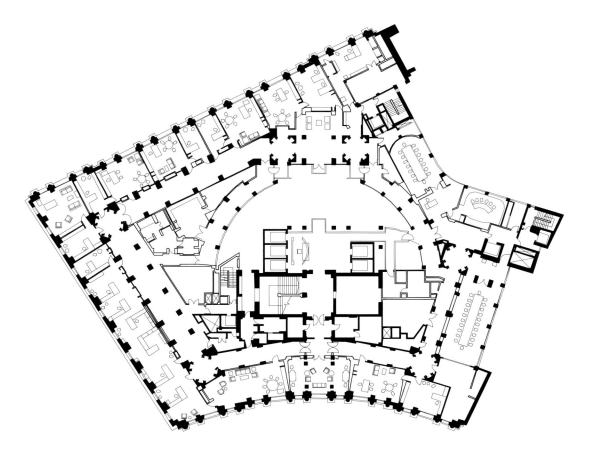

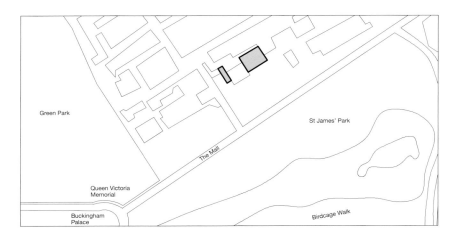

Opposite The exterior of Marlborough House showing the carefully designed extended east wing.

Marlborough House

Pall Mall, Westminster
Client: Commonwealth Secretariat
Completion: 1995

Context
Marlborough House, secure behind its high wall to The Mall, was completed in 1711 to designs by Sir Christopher Wren – his client was Sarah, Duchess of Marlborough. Little more than a century later, it became Crown property and was initially occupied by Princess Charlotte and her husband Prince Leopold. Queen Adelaide, William IV's widow, later lived there, as did Queen Alexandra following the death of her husband Edward VII and Queen Mary after the demise of George V. In 1962, following the death of Queen Mary, the building, surplus to the needs of the Royal household, was allocated to the Commonwealth Secretariat.

Brief
The house had undergone many alterations and additions after its completion by Wren, with work by, amongst others, Sir Robert Taylor and Sir William Chambers. The main block, for example, was raised by a storey and wings were added to the east and west, producing somewhat unsatisfactory results. The Commonwealth Secretariat retained the formal spaces in the main block for conferences and functions, converting the wings for office use. HOK's role was to carry out restoration work on the exterior of the building and to re-equip the wings as modern office spaces, introducing such refinements as a broadcasting studio, while greatly upgrading the services. The condition of the fabric was delicate and the routing of the extended Jubilee Line of the London Underground beneath the house was potentially a further problem. The whole project was summed up by David King, the HOK director in charge, as 'fascinating historically but technically very challenging'. The poor quality of some of the original building fabric was highlighted by a survey carried out prior to the start of works.

Solution
An analysis of the client's growing accommodation requirements revealed the need for extending the Grade I listed building if those requirements were to be met on the site. Every existing space had to be efficiently used. A former champagne cellar was adapted as a plant room while the new broadcasting studio was located in a space excavated beneath the garden, insulated to exclude noise from above and from the tube trains below.

The scope for extension was greatest in the east wing, adjoining the Royal Mews, which contained 'Wren's kitchen'. A rather awkward proposal for creating a third-floor mansard in this block had been prepared by another practice. HOK redesigned this scheme with far happier results, reusing the eighteenth-century roof trusses, and won backing from English Heritage and the then Royal Fine Art Commission, which took a close interest in the whole project. The Wren kitchen, which it had been proposed should be subdivided with a mezzanine floor, was largely retained as a double-height space with a new reception area. The central lightwell to the east block was glazed over to form a top-lit atrium.

Service cores and risers throughout the complex were rationalized to reduce their impact on the historic fabric. Partitioning in the east and west wings was removed, original room spaces restored and a higher proportion of open-plan office space created. The formal spaces in the central area were carefully repaired and restored.

Marlborough House is an outstanding example of the marriage of sensitive conservation with imaginative adaptive reuse of a historically and architecturally important building. The successful combination of authentic building fabric with carefully integrated new design elements preserves the best of the past while ensuring a continuing and purposeful use of the space for many years to come.

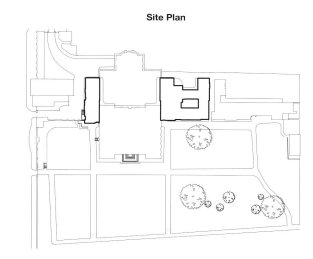

0   5   10m

Plan

Section

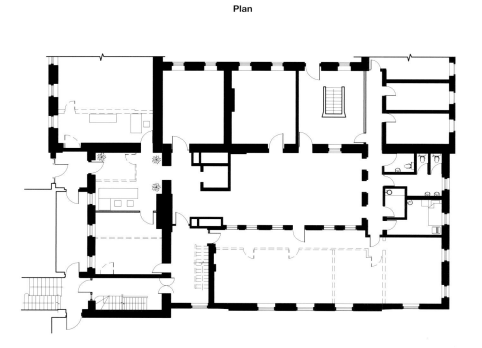

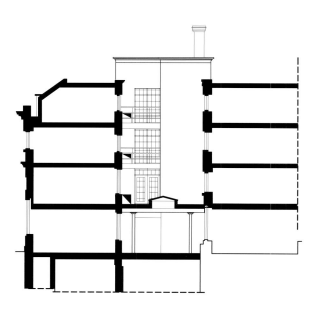

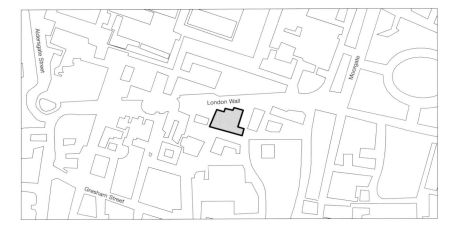

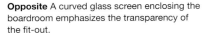

Cleary, Gottlieb, Steen & Hamilton

Basinghall Street, City of London
Client: Cleary, Gottlieb,
Steen & Hamilton
Completion: 1994

Context
The commission from Anglo-American law firm Cleary, Gottlieb, Steen & Hamilton to fit out 1,400 square metres (15,000 square feet) of office space in City Place House (a routine 1980s block) followed the Bishopsgate bombing of 1993, which necessitated the firm's move into temporary accommodation. HOK was initially responsible for a technical assessment of relocation options, followed by the development of a planning concept and interior design for the new offices.

Brief
A significant issue was the balance between the partners' cellular offices – almost always required by legal firms, and part of a culture that stresses confidentiality and privacy – and the client's wish to create a sense of openness, communication and interaction amongst its staff. Another traditional aspect of the culture of legal practice is the continuing reliance on paper – law firms maintain large paper files and also have extensive libraries.

Solution
These seemingly contradictory requirements – acoustic privacy and visual openness; plentiful paper storage and clean, efficient and elegant surroundings – formed the basis of the design concept, in which the need for privacy and soundproof partitions was met and mastered by the need for extensive document storage. Instead of building walls and placing filing cabinets and bookcases against them, HOK chose to create the walls as storage units. The density of the documents and printed material provides effective sound attenuation between rooms, whilst the timber panelling encloses these mundane 'walls' of paper.

Consistent use of glass partition screens provides a transparency that encourages communication and interaction among partners and staff. The skilful use of natural light helps to maintain a sense of openness and connectivity. The resulting design has a 'yin/yang' quality of transparency and enclosure.

Although partners retain enclosed offices along the perimeter of the building, these are essentially glazed enclosures that allow daylight to penetrate to the secretarial workstations at the centre of the floor. A generously scaled 'boulevard' separates these two areas. This combination of circulation and open-plan workplaces gives the essentially internal spaces a sense of generosity. The reception area, boardroom, library and meeting rooms are grouped to allow maximum flexibility of use, along with a sensible level of visual security provided by the reception area.

Fine finishes are a tradition of law offices, and Cleary, Gottlieb, Steen & Hamilton is no exception. The interior spaces benefit from the use of limestone flooring, which is employed in all the public and circulation areas. Pale, figured timber veneer with subtle highlights of stainless steel expresses the design vocabulary, and much of the furniture was custom-made.

0   10   20m

Plan

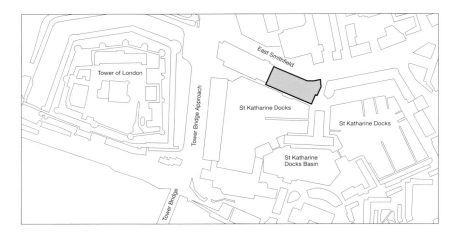

Opposite left The reception desk is located on the balcony overlooking the trading floor.

Opposite right A spiral staircase links the double-height trading floor with the balcony.

Instinet

Commodity Quay, St Katharine Docks, Tower Hamlets
Client: Instinet Ltd
Completion: 1995

Context
Instinet, the financial arm of the Reuters organization, is an electronic agency stockbroker operating internationally, with its European base in London. HOK was commissioned to fit out space at Commodity Quay, a 1960s block that forms part of St Katharine Docks, adjacent to the Tower of London. The building had been occupied by Instinet and Reuters in an ad hoc fashion, such that Instinet's operations were spread over four floors and were, consequently, somewhat disconnected.

Brief
The project began with an analysis of the company's space requirements and the development of a strategy for phased construction. The latter was required to minimize disruption to Instinet's operations and to ensure the project would be completed in less than a year. The overall design intention was to create a space in which the trading floor was the centre and focus, mirroring in physical form the organizational diagram of the client's activities.

Solution
A double-height space was created so that ancillary functions could be visually linked to the trading floor, and marketing and business development were placed on the perimeter balcony that surrounds it. Trading support and other activities operate within the same space to promote the interdepartmental interaction which was seen as vital to the business. Meeting rooms and administrative offices are located in single-storey spaces under the balcony.

The palette of materials and colours was chosen to give a fresh, crisp and contemporary feel to the space. The lightness of the interior is enhanced by the use of translucent glass panels and burnished stainless-steel details, which compensate for the relatively low level of natural illumination.

Just as speed of construction was an inherent aspect of the design, so future expansion was a fundamental consideration as well. In the event of the trading operation expanding, the ancillary activities surrounding the trading floor can be shunted elsewhere in the building and further trading desks installed with minimal disruption. The project is an early example of Aileen Asher's ability to understand the client's needs and her commitment to realizing them with grace and elegance.

0   10   50m

Third Floor Plan

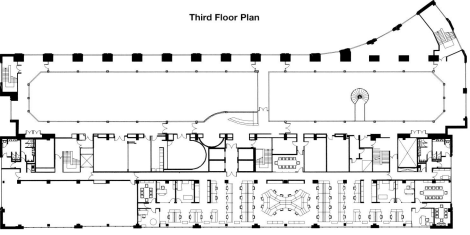

Second Floor Plan

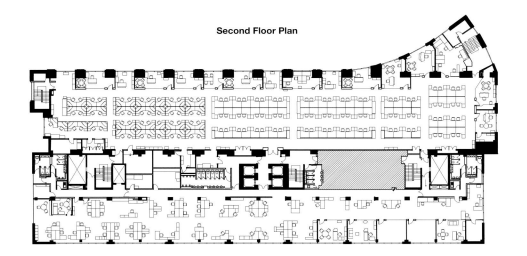

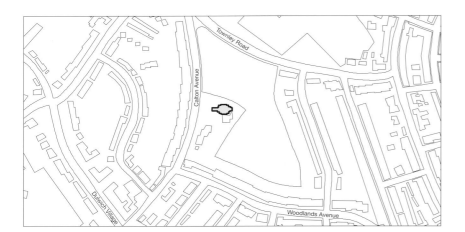

Opposite St Barnabas Church uses traditional iconography combined with contemporary materials.

St Barnabas Church

**Calton Avenue, Dulwich,
Southwark
Client: St Barnabas Parochial
Church Council
Completion: 1996**

Context

Commissions for new churches are rare in today's London: indeed, the capital has, if anything, an over-abundance of places of worship thanks to the activities of nineteenth-century church-builders. One Victorian church that remained well used and much loved was St Barnabas, Dulwich, opened in 1894; a typical example of the well-crafted Gothic style of the period realized in brick with stone dressings. Unfortunately, just before Christmas 1992 fire gutted the building, destroying the roof and everything inside and gravely weakening the surviving tower and external walls. Out of this catastrophe, however, came new life and a new church building designed by HOK.

Brief

HOK, led by design director Larry Malcic, won the project from a shortlist of three practices, the other two being specialists in church design. Malcic, a practising Roman Catholic, had designed a church in the USA but came to St Barnabas intent on learning about the special character and needs of the parish. The architects' task was to respond to a client brief that sought 'a new home for worship, prayer, learning, celebration, recreation and service to the community'. HOK's vision for the new church was that of a building that 'respected tradition but equally would be a witness to contemporary faith'. The new building, Malcic argued, should be 'flexible and welcoming, but unmistakably a church'. The old St Barnabas, with its lofty west tower, was a local landmark, and it was felt that its replacement should incorporate an element that expressed something about the Christian faith at the end of the twentieth century. The use of light, as a symbol of the divine presence, emerged as a fundamental theme in HOK's designs. These were developed in close consultation with the parish and eventually won support, after extended negotiations, from Southwark planners and English Heritage. (St Barnabas is close to the historic village centre of Dulwich.)

Solution

One basic issue was the siting of the new building. The Victorian church had abutted directly on to the street, but the new St Barnabas is set back from the road with a generous forecourt that incorporates the low foundation walls of the old church. The latter was not strictly oriented, but its successor is aligned exactly on an east/west axis. Large glazed openings invite views into the new building, especially by night when the interior as seen from the street glows invitingly. From further afield, St Barnabas is a presence on the skyline by day and night. Malcic's exploration of the theme of light found expression in the glass spire, designed in conjunction with engineer Mark Whitby of Whitby & Bird. Rising 17 metres (55 feet) above the ridge of the roof, the spire – at five tonnes – is actually a remarkably lightweight structure, formed of welded stainless steel with a delicacy that evokes the economy of Gothic architecture. Internally, the spire is located directly above the central sanctuary, which has

an octagonal altar set on a platform that can be removed should the space need to be reconfigured for a specific liturgical, cultural or community event. Organ and choir – the parish has a strong musical tradition – are placed east of the sanctuary. The planning of the building thus responds to a contemporary view of the liturgy – St Barnabas is a parish in the 'central' Anglican tradition, with the Eucharist the centre of its worship, but also open to more experimental approaches to liturgy. The skilful way in which the plan reconciles the traditional longitudinal form with the centralized emphasis that has become dominant in Roman Catholic and Anglican church design post-Vatican II is one of the great strengths of the building.

The structure of the church – in situ concrete faced in brick, with a steel-framed roof – displays a solidity and sturdiness that has roots in traditional ecclesiastical architecture and that balances the contrasting elements of lightness and transparency. Massive

brick piers enclose the worship space, which seats 430 but which can be expanded to accommodate 200 more by opening up folding screens that enclose the chapel in the western narthex (used for weekday services and private prayer), and the wing of meeting rooms and offices to the south of the church. The textured warmth of the interior of St Barnabas is generated by the use of terracotta floor tiles and vaulted ceilings of slatted beech, which contribute to its excellent acoustics. In line with the imperative for flexibility, seating can be rearranged or entirely removed as necessary. It takes the form not of chairs but of stacking benches designed by Luke Hughes (also responsible for the altar and other furnishings), which are as handsome as they are practical. Having been removed from the building beforehand, the Victorian font survived the fire and was reinstated at the west end of the new church. A significant feature of the interior is the remarkably successful stained glass in the east end and western chapel designed by Caroline

Swash, a respected artist in the field of stained glass and a member of the congregation. The old St Barnabas had contained a wealth of Victorian glass – all sadly lost in the fire. The new glass combines traditional resonances with abstract forms and rich colour, and the merit of Swash's work was recognized by a Lottery grant that helped the parish to fund its installation.

The St Barnabas project, modest in terms of its budget (around £1.5 million), might have seemed an incongruous undertaking for an international practice such as HOK. However, leaving aside Larry Malcic's own personal commitment to it, the project was important for the practice – 'it signalled the fact that we were rooted in London, here to stay', says Malcic. In fact, it was HOK's detachment from the narrow field of church design that allowed the practice to take a fresh approach to the challenge of designing a place of worship that would also be an asset for the local community. St Barnabas has

a strength and presence that recalls the best churches of the nineteenth century – most of them built of humble brick. Eschewing extraneous symbolism and decoration, it provides a numinous but practical space for praise, contemplation and celebration. If one looks for another modern church in London of which the same could be said, Maguire & Murray's noble St Paul's, Bow Common of the 1960s springs to mind – and that is high praise indeed.

Opposite View looking west with a cross made from the timbers of the previous church.

Right The organ in the choir space was designed for the church by Kenneth Tickell.

Left The slate and brick walls create an abstract base for the glass spire.

Opposite The 17-metre (56-foot) spire, designed in conjunction with Mark Whitby, is almost Gothic in its use of structure and light.

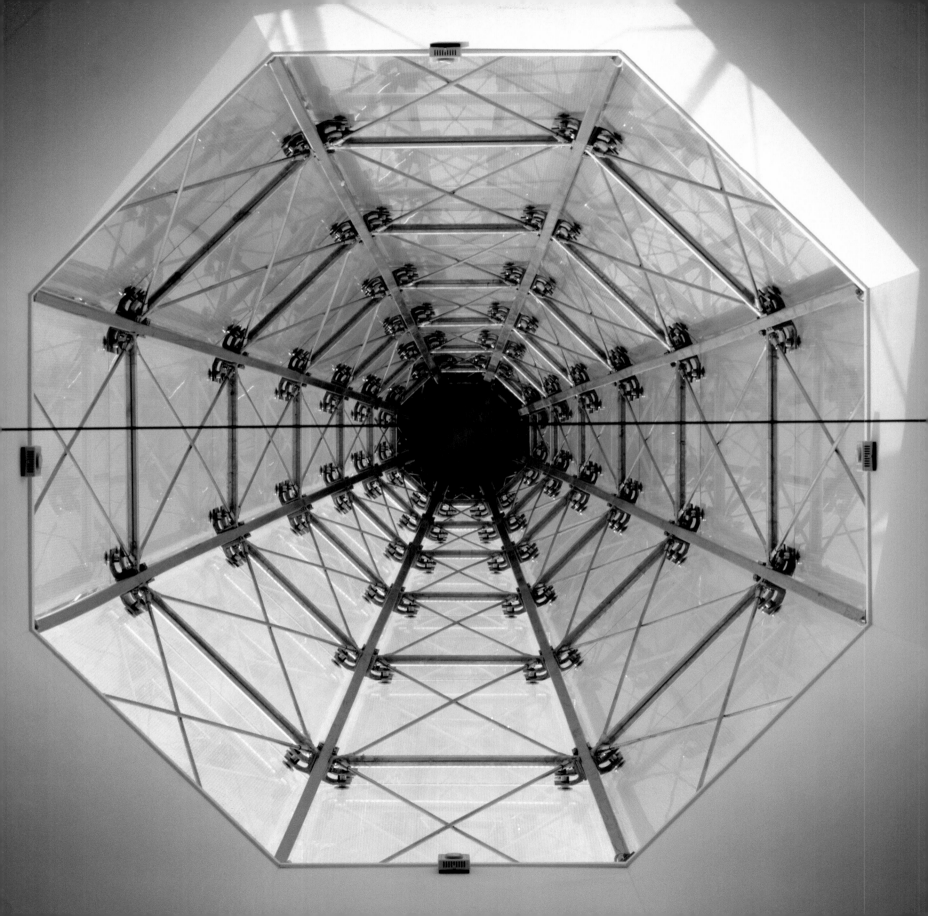

Opposite At night the church and its spire provide a beacon of faith for the community.

Site Plan

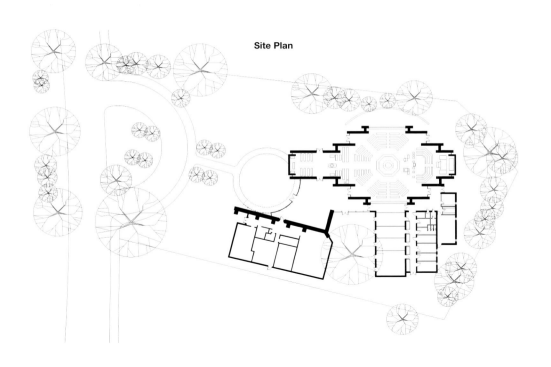

0   10   50m

Section

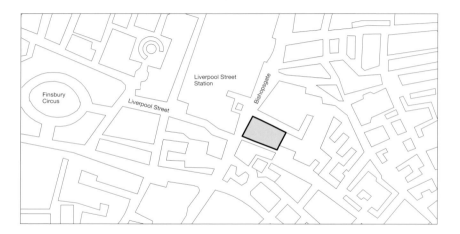

Opposite left The exterior was carefully restored and sympathetically extended.

Opposite right The interior is unquestionably contemporary.

158–164 Bishopsgate

Bishopsgate, City of London
Client: Friends Provident
Completion: 1998

Context

The constant growth and development of the City of London emphasizes the potential conflict between heritage, expansion and change. 158–164 Bishopsgate exemplifies a balanced approach to new development that respects the historic artefact whilst instilling it with new life and purpose. The opportunity to create a quality office building on an irregularly-shaped site that contained a historical, but abandoned, Victorian fire station offered many challenges.

Brief

There were originally three properties on the site – 158 and 160 were unremarkable commercial buildings and 162–164 was the old fire station, built in 1884–5, with a courtyard and outbuildings. One of several fire stations designed by George Vulliamy, Superintending Architect of the Metropolitan Board of Works, it was built in a lavish Tudor Gothic style with moulded terracotta blocks and Portland stone. It had been listed Grade II in 1972.

Solution

The site was the subject of several failed proposals, but the gradual expansion of the City and city planners encouraging retail use gave the development momentum in 1997.

Because of the layout, some valuable frontage had to be given up to service access, which had to be laid out to avoid the fourteenth-century window found in the fifteenth-century wall on the boundary. The rights to light from the overlooking buildings also had to be negotiated. Numbers 158 and 160 were demolished and replaced with a sympathetic new design that draws from its historic surroundings, without attempting to counterfeit them. It derives its proportions and sense of composition from adjacent properties, particularly the fire station, but it is a contemporary building. The design expresses twin concerns of HOK: respect for the historic fabric and context and the desire to express new buildings in contemporary yet classic forms.

The fire station was in dire need of repair. The dry rot was corrected and the building made watertight. The cast steel windows were repaired and the tall, fragile chimney stacks were stitched together and re-supported. A new office extension was built to the rear where the old outbuildings had been. The doorways where the fire engines had raced out became the shop windows for Tesco. The old newspaper kiosk, with castellated top, was recreated to form the entrance to the offices, and the front part of the basement became a wine bar.

The interior spaces were given a clean, contemporary expression that continued the idea of a building in transition. If the exterior stands astride several eras, from decorative Victorian to honest modern, then lobby and lift cores are an unabashed essay in clean modernism. It not only provides new quality office space in the city, but also firmly roots the building in its own time and place, reconciling the historic use of the site with the needs of today.

0   10   50m

Ground Floor Plan

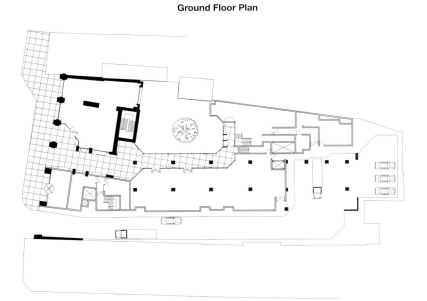

Fourth Floor Plan

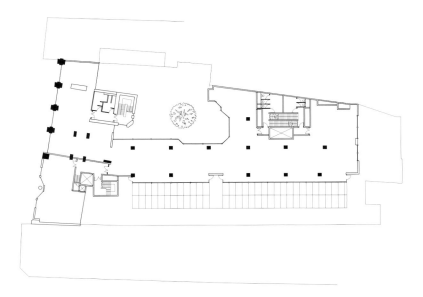

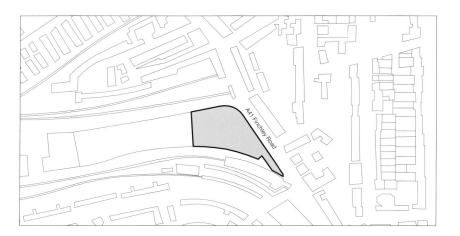

Opposite The building has a transparent quality to draw visitors in from the Finchley Road.

O₂ Centre

Finchley Road, Camden
Client: Burford Group Plc
Completion: 1998

Context

The O₂ development on Finchley Road, whose 150-metre (500-foot) long façade has become a new local landmark, is, on one level, a straightforward commercial proposition. It contains an eight-screen cinema, a leisure centre, bars, shops and restaurants – and is a hugely popular destination in this part of London, particularly for the young. The style of the 'operation' is slick, even brash, and tailored to the market. On another level, however, the project is an exercise in urban regeneration. The site – close to Finchley Road Station and adjacent to the rail tracks that carry trains out of Baker Street and Marylebone – was, with its few poor-quality shop units on Finchley Road, largely derelict, its former industrial use having long ceased.

Brief

The site sat empty for more than a decade as succeeding owners and developers sought to define an appropriate use for the property. A new developer-client was exploring possible mixes of uses when HOK was brought in, and the practice helped define the idea of an 'urban entertainment centre'. In effect this was a new building type, though it has since been widely taken up. In recent decades, leisure activities – including health clubs and multiplex cinemas – have gravitated to the urban periphery, where they are accessible only by car. The negative impact of these developments in environmental terms is clear, but, equally, such out-of-town locations exclude non-drivers, including the young.

Solution

As the scheme evolved, the balance of uses changed. Some of the proposed restaurant spaces on upper levels were developed as retail units instead. In structural terms, the project was complex. A swimming pool, for example, is located on an upper floor. The supermarket provider demanded large, column-free spaces, while the cinema posed yet another challenge.

The role of the development as a local forum is augmented by the provision of a community hall, which has become a popular venue for weddings, bar mitzvahs and other celebrations. The detailing has been carefully considered, using high-quality materials, and the development benefits from the generous provision of natural light. The result is a straightforward, frankly commercial project – but one that is enlightened in its approach to city life. The design anticipated a new urban phenomenon and created an important centre for youth and community: its eclectic architecture and overt 'theming' are the stage-setting in which young people meet and gather. Perhaps the only disappointment of the project is its lack of connection to the Underground, despite its proximity to the nearest station, Finchley Road. Later developments building on the success of O₂, for example at Fulham Broadway, have capitalized on their public transport links.

Left and opposite The central rotunda is naturally lit and generously planted, and provides access to the multiplex cinema and restaurants at first floor level.

Opposite The generous dimensions and overt theatricality have created a popular mecca for young people.

Right Illuminated fountains and dramatic lighting emphasize the vertical circulation.

0 10   50m

Ground Floor Plan

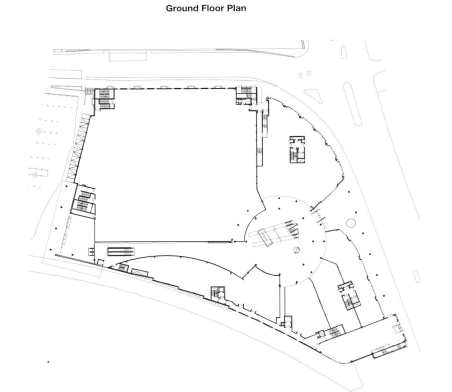

First Floor Plan

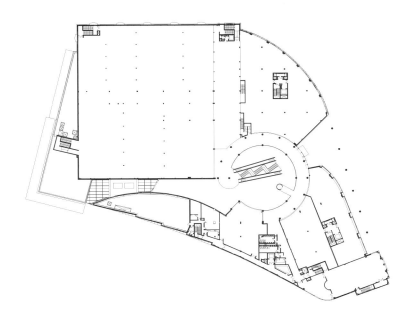

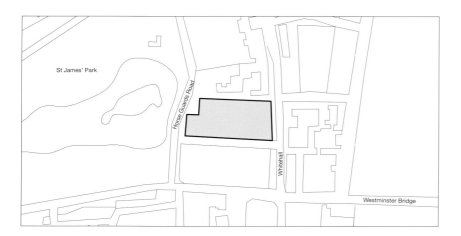

St James' Park

Horse Guards Road

Whitehall

Westminster Bridge

Foreign & Commonwealth Office

**Whitehall, Westminster
Client: The Foreign &
Commonwealth Office
Completion: 1997**

Context
Revered today as a masterpiece of Victorian architecture and decoration, the Foreign Office was, for a century or more, one of London's more controversial landmarks. Controversy began even before the imposing – and now Grade I listed – palazzo on Whitehall was constructed. Following the decision in 1856 by Lord Palmerston's government to commission purpose-built offices which were, in due course, to house not only the Foreign Office but also the India, Colonial and Home Offices, an international architectural competition was held. It was won by HE Coe, a pupil of George Gilbert Scott, but, by 1858, Coe's scheme had been abandoned by a short-lived Tory government, and a Gothic design by Scott (placed third in the competition) substituted. With the return to power of the Whig, Palmerston, Scott was obliged to abandon his beloved Gothic and redesign his scheme in an Italianate manner. The Foreign Office project thus became a famous chapter in the nineteenth-century 'battle of the styles'.

Built in phases from 1863 onwards – with the Foreign and India Offices on the east side of the site, overlooking St James's Park, ready for occupation by the end of 1867 – the entire complex was finally completed in 1874. A further complication was provided by the imposition of Matthew Digby Wyatt as Scott's collaborator on the India Office portion of the complex, though the collaboration seems to have been surprisingly amicable. Disposed around a large central court, the building is elaborately decorated both externally and internally – with the Foreign Office and former India Office portions rich in carved and painted decoration, and costly materials liberally used in the principal spaces. After the Second World War, with the India Office wound up, the Foreign Office – today the Foreign & Commonwealth Office (FCO) – gradually gained control of the entire building. The Home Office finally moved out in 1978.

By the mid 1960s, however, the entire complex was dismissed as a 'white elephant' and was scheduled for demolition as part of a comprehensive redevelopment plan for Whitehall drawn up by Sir Leslie Martin. The proposals were scrapped in 1971, though it was more than a decade before the decision was taken to carry out a thorough restoration of what had become 'a magnificent slum'. In 1982, the practice of Cecil Denny Highton, subsequently merged with HOK, was appointed as architect for a phased restoration project that extended over the next 15 years and cost more than £100 million.

Brief
The brief was, of course, not simply to repair and restore a magnificent, if neglected, historic monument but to make the building work efficiently as a modern government department. In the 1870s, the Foreign Office had employed no more than 200 people; now the FCO wanted accommodation for 2,000 staff. Antiquated services were to be renewed throughout, and the FCO was to remain in occupation as work continued, so that staff had to be decanted around

the site – the departure of the Home Office provided vital space for this purpose. The project drew, in fact, on some of HOK's key strengths, notably the practice's sense of history and place and its sure understanding, based on detailed research and analysis, of the way buildings work – or should work – for their users.

Neil Cooke, who leads HOK's conservation team, recalls the state of parts of the building in the early 1980s. He notes, for example, how Digby Wyatt's magnificent, glass-roofed Durbar Court, where John Gielgud and Peggy Ashcroft performed a scene from Romeo and Juliet at a glittering reception for the French President on the eve of the Second World War, was now filled with wooden huts, its marble floor lost under layers of pigeon droppings. The grandest of the rooms in the Locarno Suite (named after the treaty signed here in 1925) was subdivided with partitions to create a series of small, claustrophobic offices opening off a tunnel-like central corridor, while the adjacent dining room was used as a furniture store. Elsewhere, even where original spaces and decor remained essentially intact, everything was obscured by layers of dirt, coal fires having been used to heat the offices well into the early 1970s. Much of the splendid Clayton & Bell decoration on the grand staircase, the finest of the interior spaces designed by Scott, had been covered up. The imposing ground-floor vestibule of the former India Office was used as a post room. The original painted decoration had been toned down and partly obscured even in the Foreign Secretary's own office overlooking St James's Park and Horse Guards Road, from which, in 1914, Lord Grey had famously watched a lamplighter extinguishing a streetlight below and imagined 'the lamps going out all over Europe'.

Solution
As Neil Cooke notes, 'an element of reinvention' was needed in parts of the interior. The decorative features of the grand Locarno reception room, for instance, had been virtually obliterated in 1926. A painstaking search found one area in which some original paintwork survived, allowing the architects – working with specialist restorers Campbell Smith & Co. – to develop a colour scheme for authentic reinstatement. The roundels depicting signs of the zodiac were also restored in the spirit of the lost originals. Extraordinarily, one of the original gas light fittings, presumed destroyed, had been shipped to South America and later bought by the Wallace Collection in London; it provided a model for the new electric light fittings. The revived splendour of these rooms is enhanced by the use of modern technology, seamlessly woven into the restoration: fibre-optic lighting illuminating the vaulted ceiling, and underfloor heating replacing unsightly radiators – innovations of which a progressive Victorian like Scott would surely have approved. A less well-known, but nonetheless delightful interior, the FCO (formerly the Colonial Office) Library, has been sensitively extended and re-equipped for an age in which digital, as well as printed, information has to be accommodated. As part of the restoration, a stuffed anaconda presented by a missionary at the end of the nineteenth century, since which time it has hung in the library, was itself removed for restoration. The return of the reptile, carried into the building across the pavement from Whitehall, reportedly aroused considerable interest from passing tourists.

By redesigning services, utilizing under-used spaces and relocating activities – and adding a discreet rooftop extension, invisible from street level – HOK managed to increase by 20 per cent the area of usable space inside the building. Its place as a well-loved London landmark assured, the Foreign Office has been restored and renewed as both a practical workplace and an imposing symbol of Britain's continuing role in international diplomacy in a post-colonial age.

Opposite left North side of the central court.

Opposite right Entrance loggia.

Right Matthew Digby Wyatt's Durbar Court with original iron and glass roof restored and reglazed.

Preceding page left Entrance to the former Secretary of State for India's suite.

Preceding page right The Royal Stair in the former Colonial Office.

Left The grand Locarno reception room with lost painted decoration now restored.

Opposite The historic library showing the restored anaconda.

Opposite Domed ceiling of the Muses staircase designed by Matthew Digby Wyatt – the cherubs represent Roman Virtues.

Below The Foreign Secretary's Office shown after total restoration.

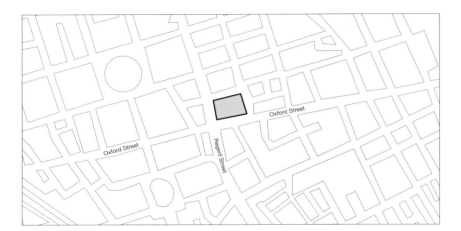

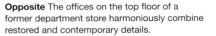
HOK London Office

Oxford Street, Westminster
Client: HOK International Ltd
Completion: 1999

Context
The rapid expansion of HOK's operations in London in the late1990s led to an urgent need for new and more spacious office accommodation. The move to 216 Oxford Street, at the north-east corner of Oxford Circus, was the outcome – although the fourth-floor space that was originally designed for 150 staff now houses over 200 people.

The offices occupy an entire storey – around 2,300 square metres (25,000 square feet) – of the former Peter Robinson department store. This Grade II listed building was designed before the First World War by Sir Henry Tanner, as part of his scheme for the Oxford Street/Regent Street quadrant, and built in 1923–4 with an extension by Hall & Clarkson along Oxford Street. Constructed on a steel frame, the store was clad in the stone Classical detailing typical of Regent Street. For a time, one of the retail landmarks of the West End, Peter Robinson (founded in 1833) contracted after the Second World War, during which the building had

suffered damage in an air raid, and only the ground, first floor and basement levels of the building are now used for retailing. In the late 1960s, Sir George Martin adapted space on the fourth floor, formerly occupied by the BBC, for use as a recording studio. The Beatles, David Bowie, Elton John and other famous names recorded there before the studio was finally closed in 1993. The space is now HOK's London base.

Brief
This level of the building once housed Peter Robinson's restaurant (along the western edge), a glamorous vaulted space decorated by the little-known Scottish mural painter George Murray with 'scenes out of the operas' – Carmen, Lohengrin, Faust, Pagliacci, Cavalleria Rusticana, Madame Butterfly and Rigoletto were all featured. Since this section of the building formed part of Martin's Air studio the murals were treated with scant respect, and areas were covered with graffiti – including signatures of some of the stars working there. When the building became

empty, souvenir hunters moved in and tore off strips of the artwork bearing the signatures. The restoration of the murals was an important element in the conversion project for the space. Since HOK's conservation team was at the time working on the Foreign & Commonwealth Office project (see pages 58–67) with specialist conservators from the firm of Campbell Smith, the latter were brought in to restore Murray's damaged murals, recreating areas that had been lost.

Solution
Having restored those elements that were sufficiently interesting and intact, HOK, led by Stephen McGrane and design director Larry Malcic, took the bold decision to treat the majority of the space as a blank canvas in which to insert contemporary, free-standing screens and rooms. The judicious use of sanded, limed plywood, lacquered MDF and a few bold colours in an otherwise white space provides economical yet memorable details and exhibits the architects'

Top left Detail of barrel-vaulted ceiling – areas that had been lost were skilfully recreated.

Bottom left The reception area, showing the mix of historic structure and new interventions.

Opposite Contemporary walls made of limed plywood do not attempt to conceal the existing building services.

HOK INTERNATIONAL LIMITED

ability to achieve high-quality finishes with humble materials. The contrast between the Edwardian grandeur and contemporary simplicity is heightened by some dramatic juxtapositions.

HOK's approach, was to leave the concrete-and-steel – almost industrial – interior very much as found, so that users benefit from very generous six-metre (20-foot) ceiling heights and an abundance of natural light. Having everyone in the same office leads to easy communications – there is 'one floor, one culture'. Meeting rooms are arranged along the southern, Oxford Street, elevation. There are virtually no enclosed offices, and the space is ideal for team-working. Rooflights and a lightwell bring daylight into the centre of the floor plan. Service ducts have been left exposed, reinforcing the raw, industrial ethos. Clients who come here for the first time often find the experience revelatory. This is an inspirational atelier, raised above the noise and constant movement of Oxford Street.

Opposite Barrel-vaulted interior of the former restaurant, now successfully converted to offices with the original decoration restored.

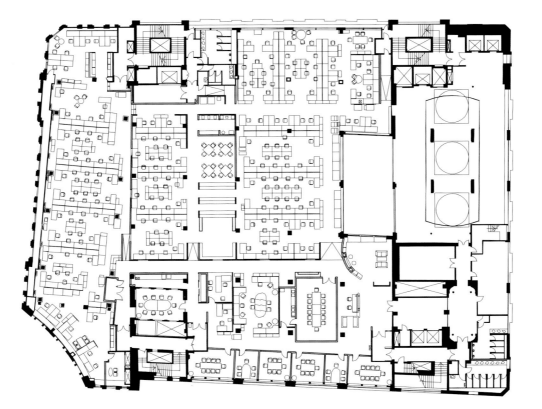

0   10   50m

Floor Plan

Tower 42

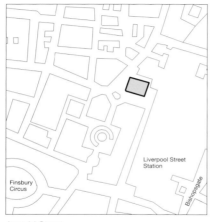

Appold Street

Opposite left In Tower 42, the interiors convey a reassuring sense of permanence.

Opposite right With sustainability in mind, building and furniture components were re-used in a new configuration.

Deutsche Bank

**Tower 42 and Appold Street,
City of London
Client: Deutsche Bank
Completion: 2000 and 2004**

Context

HOK was initially appointed in 2000 to design 560 square metres (6,000 square feet) of offices for the venture capital group of Deutsche Bank on the 40th floor of Tower 42 – formerly the NatWest Tower, and still the City of London's tallest building to date. (The practice has worked on the fit-out of a number of spaces in this landmark building.) In 2004, HOK was again commissioned by Deutsche Bank, this time to fit out space at Appold Street for the bank's asset management and controlling departments. The client requirements for these two projects were to differ in significant ways, reflecting the radical change in working practices that had occurred during the intervening period.

Brief

The brief for Tower 42 requested both open-plan and cellular office space (with ten private offices for executives) and a meeting suite. Meanwhile, the Appold Street project was to be the first to implement 'DBSmart' strategy in the UK. This strategy, which had been developed by Deutsche Bank and the Fraunhofer Institute for Applied Information Technology, aims to make efficient use of the bank's estate by rationalizing the tools its staff needed to work efficiently and defining the environment most conducive to the company's management processes, while balancing these against the aspirations of the workforce.

Solution

In Tower 42, the cellular offices have glazed fronts to ensure a sense of communication. The meeting suite has a fully soundproofed central sliding partition so that the space can be divided up when necessary, and is equipped with a state-of-the-art audio-visual system, including a 50-inch plasma screen. Bespoke joinery and the use of limestone and slate flooring in the reception area provide the element of quality demanded by the client.

At Appold Street, by contrast, the application of the DBSmart principles led to the offices being equipped with functional workstations and study booths – the latter provided for use when aural privacy is required. There is also a selection of formal and informal meeting rooms, able to accommodate from four to 12 persons, which can be booked for team meetings, training and workshops. Refreshment, 'touchdown' and lounge spaces complete with small libraries help to fulfil the desire of the staff for various supporting services.

As a result of these changes to working practices, the occupancy level of the Appold Street space was increased by 27 per cent. Sustainability was emphasized by reusing most of the existing interior elements: partitioning, ceilings, lighting, furniture and carpets were all given a new lease of life by the skilful addition of vivid colour and subtle graphics. New feature elements highlight where support services can be found, and help to provide a sense of place and identity in this highly efficient workplace.

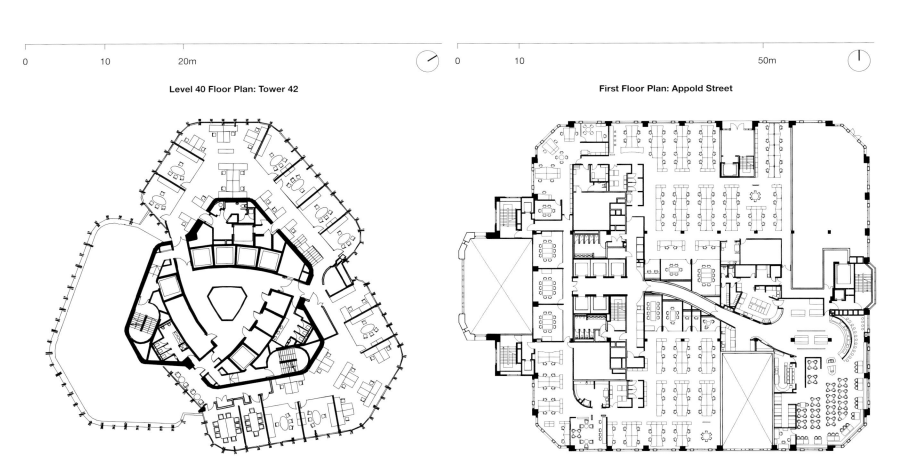

0   10   20m

Level 40 Floor Plan: Tower 42

0   10   50m

First Floor Plan: Appold Street

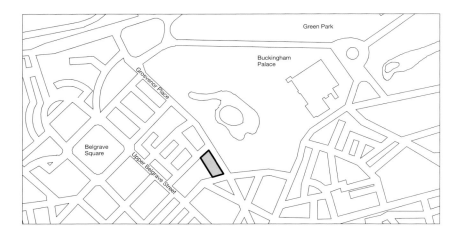

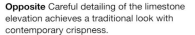

Opposite Careful detailing of the limestone elevation achieves a traditional look with contemporary crispness.

Forty Grosvenor Place

Grosvenor Place, Westminster
Client: Grosvenor Estate Holdings
Completion: 1999

Context
Nearly a decade after its completion, HOK's Forty Grosvenor Place remains an impressive exemplar, firstly of the way in which a large modern office building can be inserted into a sensitive historic environment and, secondly, of environmentally progressive design – to the extent that the project anticipated concerns that have come to the fore in Britain only in the new century.

The site, close to Victoria Railway Station and facing the enclosing wall of Buckingham Palace, was occupied by a large and undistinguished office block, Hobart House, built during the late 1930s. It is on the eastern edge of the urban quarter of Belgravia – developed in the nineteenth century by the Grosvenor Estate, which remains the freeholder, exercising a close, and benign, control over development in the area – still the most prestigious residential location in London. In this instance, the Estate's development arm was the client for the scheme and was determined to balance commercial viability with a development that was in tune with the character of the surrounding area.

Brief
HOK won the £52 million project in competition in 1995 (from a shortlist that included the practices of Terry Farrell, Michael Hopkins and Richard MacCormac). The client brief reflected extensive research into the office market in this sector of the West End, with its distinctive profile – very different from that of the City or Docklands. In West End terms, at 30,000 square metres (325,000 square feet), 40 Grosvenor Place is a rare beast – sites for buildings on this scale are relatively scarce in the heart of the City of Westminster. The development was seen as potentially having a broad appeal, with British-based, European and American businesses as possible tenants. However, northern European norms in office design include access to natural light for all users, while American businesses generally expect large, clear floorplates. Equally, there was the possibility that the entire building might be let to a single user or that it might be subdivided, with legal businesses for example, demanding largely cellular offices, and financial operations requiring expanses of open-plan space. The emphasis from the start, therefore, was very much on flexibility. Dispersed service cores, with staircases and WCs, and the provision of four distinct lift cores allowed for the building to be occupied by four separate tenants. (In the event, the whole building was pre-let to a multinational corporation but is now multi-tenanted – a transition that was achieved painlessly.)

Solution
Both the Grosvenor Estate and the Westminster planners were concerned that the development should relate not only to the character of Grosvenor Place, with its large commercial buildings, but also to the adjacent residential streets and conservation areas. A highly transparent look, with large expanses of glazing, was

ruled out. The building is faced in a creamy limestone that relates well to the stuccoed terraces of Belgravia, with a relatively high proportion of wall surface to window openings – the latter featuring glass fins to eliminate solar heat gain. A curved pavilion, a modern interpretation of a typically Regency device, addresses the junction of Grosvenor Place and Hobart Place. By breaking down the three street façades into a series of vertical planes, each symmetrical in its own right, and emphasizing the first floor as a piano nobile with extended window openings, the architects provided a further link to the historic context, although there are no overt historicist references. (The building relates well to the adjacent Portland stone façades of 25–35 Grosvenor Place, a mid-1950s project by Sir Albert Richardson and a good, if late, example of 'progressive Classicism'.)

The focus of the building internally is the central atrium, or 'forum', expressing the idea of Forty

Grosvenor Place as an urban village in microcosm, with a restaurant, brasserie, staff café, retail units and conference centre (the latter now converted to offices) disposed around the perimeter. A health club is located at basement level, while a concierge service provides a wide range of services for tenants – it can, for example, book cabs or secure tickets for West End theatres. Since the lift cores are accessed from the atrium, all the building's users must pass through this space, creating a sense of community and an ethos of 'live/work/play'. Initially, the atrium was configured as a covered 'garden under glass', but the planting has now been reduced and a central fountain removed. The west wall of the space is entirely glazed, providing views out to adjoining gardens and the Greek Revival church tower of St Peter's, Eaton Square. This glazed wall is in tune with the metal-and-glass aesthetic of the atrium, but the planners were resistant to the idea of a highly reflective external surface facing

St Peter's and the square beyond. Accordingly, HOK, working with engineer Whitby Bird and Partners, developed a structural system based on 40-metre (130-foot) long Vierendeel trusses, the structural elements placed externally to provide the requisite element of solidity. The impressive atrium is a naturally ventilated, daylit space, designed to be publicly accessible – though recent concerns about security have restricted access. Office floors are typically of 3,000 square metres (33,000 square feet) but, thanks to the introduction of secondary atria through the upper floors, no workspace is further than eight metres (25 feet) from a source of natural light – a clear response to progressive, European standards of workplace design.

Forty Grosvenor Place is a highly innovative project that was completed to a moderate budget. The construction strategy combined an in situ concrete frame with loadbearing façades of pre-cast concrete – eliminating the

need for perimeter columns, allowing maximum flexibility in internal fit-out, reducing construction time and hence producing significant cost savings. The aim from the start was to produce a low-energy building that set new environmental standards. The sustainable agenda of the project was developed in collaboration with Arup, and includes the use of chilled ceilings combined with displacement ventilation at floor level (eliminating the need for ductwork and fans). The atrium is warmed in winter by exhaust heat from the floorplates. In summer it is naturally ventilated by the stack effect, and it forms a natural buffer between the external climate and the office floors. Finally, the limited use of glass in the external façades is a major element in reducing energy consumption and another aspect of the project's forward-looking agenda.

As design director Larry Malcic describes it, Forty Grosvenor Place 'conserves natural resources while it enhances human resources',

Opposite left The contrast between the limestone and steel elements emphasizes the different parts of the building.

Opposite right 40-metre (130-foot) glass wall inside the atrium.

Right Painted steel Vierendeel trusses recall the heroic engineering of the nineteenth century.

creating a progressive workplace within an envelope of simple, classic elegance. Within a large team, project designers Christopher Colosimo and Gordon Cobban worked with Malcic to develop the uniquely adaptable building plan and a highly articulate set of details in which the ornament of the building is a direct, authentic expression of the stone, steel and glass used in its construction.

At Forty Grosvenor Place, HOK set out to create an office building for the twenty-first century: a building that was not only functional in business terms but that was also the focus for a working community and connected to the wider community beyond its walls. The project advanced the notion of the office building as a 'club' or 'campus', where human interaction is recognized as the key ingredient in generating business success.

Opposite and right The atrium with its café is naturally heated and cooled. Its garden under glass is a microcosm of Belgravia.

Below left The forum space provides generous natural lighting within the office spaces.

Below right The boardroom foyer uses sustainable weathered sycamore veneer to reinforce the theme of classic elegance.

Bottom left The café provides a social focus for the firm.

Bottom right Conference suite rooms with full-height glazing encourage a sense of community.

Opposite The steel that supports the lift lobbies, lifts and bridges provides the only ornament in the atrium.

Opposite The corner turrets emphasize the building's relationship to the conservation areas surrounding it.

0   10   50m

Third Floor Plan

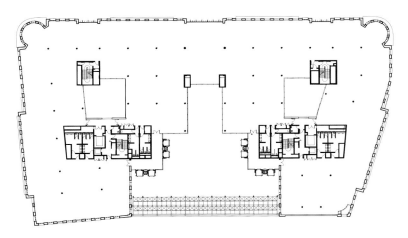

First Floor Plan

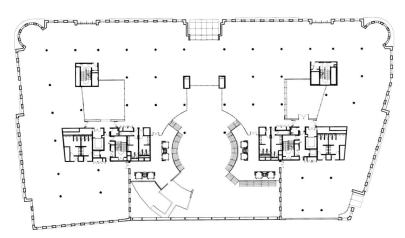

Section

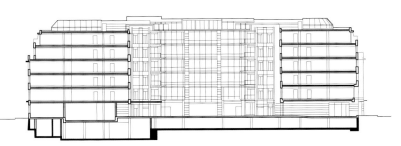

Ground Floor Plan

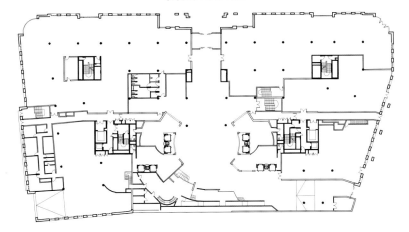

Northwest Elevation

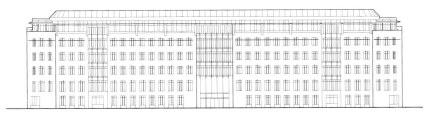

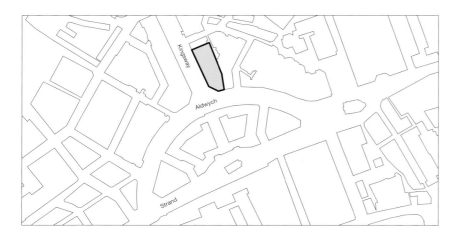

Opposite Entrance security was embedded into the base building aesthetic.

ExxonMobil – St Catherine's House

Kingsway, Westminster
Client: ExxonMobil Corporation
Completion: 2000

Context

Mobil (which merged with Exxon halfway through the project) commissioned HOK in 1998 to fit out its new headquarters at St Catherine's House. This is a large 1920s block in Kingsway, which at the time was being totally rebuilt behind a retained façade with two atria as the focal points of its new interior.

Brief

The brief called for 17,000 square metres (180,000 square feet) of office space on nine floors of the building, with both open-plan and cellular accommodation. At the entrance level, light-filled atria were to be developed as interactive spaces for staff to meet or just relax over a coffee.

Solution

HOK's interior masterplan responded to the company's workspace strategy. The initial brief was for only a small element of cellular offices (5 per cent of the total requirement). Post-merger, however, Exxon demanded a very different mix – 40 per cent of the office space became cellular in form. The retention of break-out and 'touchdown' spaces nonetheless reflected a willingness to explore new ways of working. Cellular offices were generally located around the two atria, thus avoiding the juxtaposition of modular spaces with the non-uniform building perimeter. Security was a significant issue for the client – a glazed screen, with provision for smoke-ducting in the event of a fire, enclosed the ground-floor reception area. Colour, lighting and appropriate furnishings helped create a prestige headquarters, which reflected the strength of the client's brand.

The variation in sill levels and the proportions of the existing window openings in the retained façade imbued each storey with an individual character, which was further enhanced by the introduction of distinctive colours at each floor level to facilitate 'wayfinding'. 'Earth', 'Water', 'Air' and 'Fire' were adopted as inspirational themes, and these were reflected in the choice of floor and wall finishes and furnishings. Elliptical vestibules in neutral hues linked lift lobbies to the office floors, and provided a serene transition between vertical and horizontal circulation. A fully equipped kitchen and staff restaurant, which included a servery with 'theatre cooking', was included at ground-floor level.

The design provided a strong conceptual plan that was executed with liveliness and panache.

Opposite The transparency of the atrium was echoed in the fit-out.

Right The 'touchdown' provided visiting staff members with access to emails and correspondence within the atrium space.

Far right The boardroom was enhanced by simple but dramatic lighting.

0   10   50m

Typical Floor Plan

Ground Floor Plan

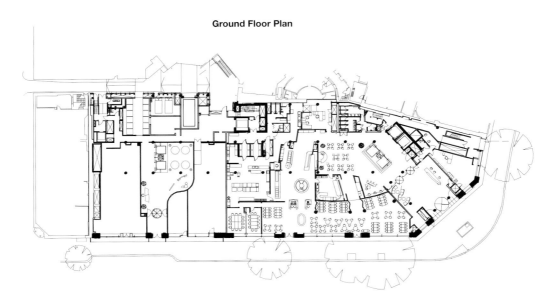

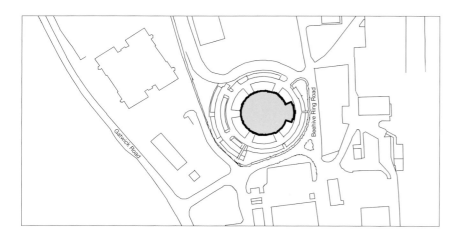

The Beehive Building

Gatwick Airport, West Sussex
Client: BAA Lynton
Completion: 1999

Context

One of the prime reasons for the growth of Gatwick, first opened as one of London's airports in 1936, was its proximity to the main railway line between London and Brighton. Even in the 1930s Gatwick was just 40 minutes from Victoria Station, making it more convenient than Croydon, then London's principal airport. At Gatwick, a railway station was opened close to the runway and was directly connected by a 120-metre (400-foot) long subway to the new terminal building – 'the most modern and practical air terminus in Great Britain', as it was described on its opening – which is now known as The Beehive.

Today, The Beehive is a rare surviving example of a pre-war British airport building, and is listed Grade II. Designed by architects Hoar, Marlow & Lovett, the building is circular in form and constructed largely of reinforced concrete. The circular plan was envisaged as a model for the airports of the future, but was not pursued in post-

war civil aviation projects. Internally, the terminal featured a spacious passenger concourse, entered directly from the subway, surrounded by a ring of lounges and offices, with an outer ring catering for customs and freight dispatch. Six corridors led from the concourse to the aircraft, with retractable canopies offering shelter from the weather. The control tower sat neatly at the centre of the circle with a clear view of the runways, overlooked by a public viewing terrace capable of seating 100 visitors. Elegantly detailed in modernistic style, The Beehive was an excellent example of a new building type of the inter-war period. With the development of Gatwick's new terminals from the 1950s onwards, however, it became redundant and was let to a series of small businesses. Under-maintained, it clearly needed a permanent new use.

Brief

HOK's task was to convert the listed structure in order to house offices for GB Airways – originally Gibraltar-based,

but since 1989 run from Britain with extensive operations out of Gatwick. The Beehive provided ample space for the company's requirements in an ideal location. The challenge was to retain the original character of the building while equipping it for its new function, and extended discussions took place with English Heritage as the conversion project was developed by a team led by John Andrew.

Solution

The first priority was one of repair, since the roof in particular was in poor condition and the rooflights had been covered over, excluding daylight. English Heritage wanted to retain the integrity of the original spaces. In such a relatively small building keeping the concourse as found might have seemed a luxury, but the space is partly occupied by a well-used café. In addition, a new entrance has been created since the subway is no longer in use (although it still exists). In the remainder of the building, spaces had to be provided for GB Airways'

Left Sweeping curves of the reception desk mirror the overall plan of the building.

Right The restored exterior of Gatwick's first airport terminal.

Bottom right Portals and glass recall the original Art Deco fittings of the building.

various departments, and these were conceived by HOK as working 'neighbourhoods'. Offices around the circumference of the concourse have been enclosed with translucent glass, providing for privacy while not excluding natural light from the top-lit central space – now with its original rooflights reinstated. The central core of the building contains meeting rooms enclosed with glass bricks. Original details were retained and restored: for example, the stylish brass handrails to the staircases. The control tower has been retained intact, but current health and safety issues rule out its being put to any practical use for the foreseeable future. In every other respect, the project represents a remarkably precise fit between historical fabric and the needs of a modern business.

Opposite The internal fit-out capitalized on natural light by using translucent and glass block partitions.

0   10   50m

First Floor Plan

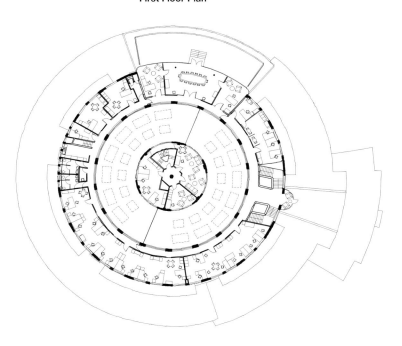

Ground Floor Plan

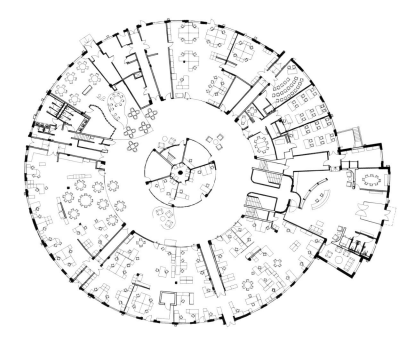

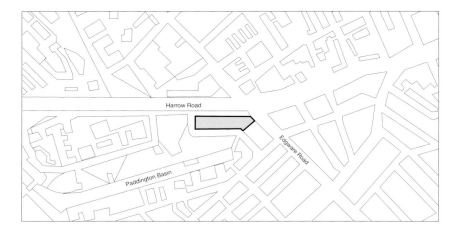

Harrow Road

Edgware Road

Paddington Basin

Opposite, left to right Unusually for a hotel the elevations have a depth of complexity that conceals the simple grid of windows that typically identifies a hotel.

Hilton Metropole Hotel

Edgware Road, Westminster
Client: Hilton International
Completion: 2000

Context
The original London Metropole Hotel on Edgware Road was one of a number in London designed by the ubiquitous Richard Seifert as part of the hotel boom of the 1960s and early 1970s. It was large and prominent, located within easy reach of the West End, on a main route into London and close to Paddington Station. The hotel was much extended in the early 1990s, but its present form is the result of a far more ambitious extension and reconstruction project by HOK.

Brief
The brief was to make the Hilton Metropole the largest hotel in London – an extra 440 guest rooms formed part of the scheme. The context for these proposals was the projected transformation of the area, following the opening of the fast rail link from Paddington Station to Heathrow Airport, and the development of the long-desolate Paddington Basin, as a mixed-use urban quarter with apartments and high-quality office space.

Solution
Obtaining the space needed for the requisite new accommodation meant utilizing the site to the full, but there were severe constraints: major roads on the surface and the Underground below, with the canal basin forming a boundary to the west. In addition, the hotel had to remain in use during construction work. HOK's scheme was an ingenious exercise in squeezing the maximum use out of precious, limited space by building both up and down from street level.

The new guest rooms were contained within a steel-framed extension, carried on 5-metre (17-foot) deep trusses spanning the site – two rooms were accommodated between each pair of trusses. The new block had something of the character of a ship – the lower floors forming the 'hull'; with big, column-free ballroom and banqueting spaces, independently serviced, as a 'superstructure'. (Heavy-duty lifts were installed: product launches are a speciality of the hotel, and entire trucks can be now conveyed to the upper floors.) Below ground, the greatly extended kitchen spaces were housed in what had been parking areas. Further space was obtained by cantilevering floors out over pavements – in fact, there was a public gain here, since these provided shelter from the down-draughts that Seifert's tower had always generated.

The entire building was, in effect, repackaged, giving it a sleek new look. Many hotels of the 1960s tended to have an 'egg box' look. HOK's aim here was to create a smooth, but lively, aesthetic. The fully glazed façade forms a tight thermal enclosure, with a mix of fitted glazing, aluminium and granite providing a sense of animation, layering and solar shading (carried on the structural steel frame), which reinforces the environmental strategy. There are excellent views of the basin area from the upper floors. The technical challenge was enormous, but the results have enhanced an area that is finally realizing its hidden potential.

0   10   50m

Ground Floor Plan

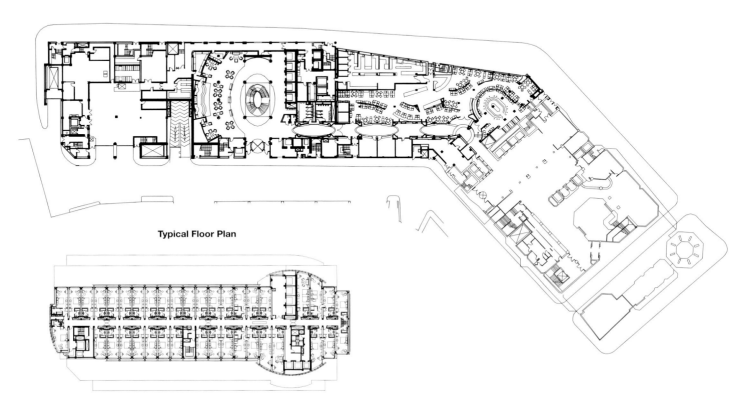

Typical Floor Plan

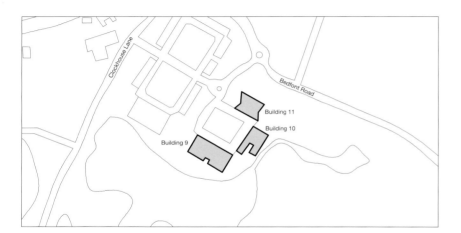

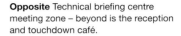

Cisco Bedfont Lakes

Feltham, Hounslow, Middlesex
Client: Cisco Systems
Completion: 2001

Context

HOK's interiors team, led by Aileen Asher, had completed fit-out projects for Cisco Systems in Paris and Brussels before undertaking this 25,000 square metre (270,000 square foot) project at Bedfont Lakes, a business park near London's Heathrow Airport.

Brief

Intended to house sales and marketing staff for the company's UK operation and to act as their British headquarters, Cisco's offices at Bedfont Lakes are housed in three mid-rise blocks (Buildings 9, 10 and 11), each planned around a central atrium. The staff based here actually spend the majority of their time outside their offices, where they can use workstations in open-plan areas or plug into power and data ports provided in more informal spaces around the buildings.

Solution

The company's own buildings deliberately make use of the most advanced technology and act as an exemplar for potential clients. The main reception area at Bedfont Lakes (in Building 9) is aimed at the latter, with a sophisticated presentation of Cisco's products using graphics, a 16-screen media wall and interactive 'totems'. Adjacent to reception, the executive briefing centre – based on the one at the company's world headquarters in San Jose, California – contains demonstration labs and conference spaces. Building 9 also has a restaurant and training centre; the two other blocks act as 'satellites', housing conferencing and meeting spaces as well as small cafés.

Completed to a strict budget and tight schedule, and in close liaison with the client's own facilities managers, the Cisco project embodies devices successfully used by HOK in other interiors projects. Colour is used freely and boldly to animate the spaces and create a sense of place and identity. Lift lobbies are conceived as 'gateways'; circular spaces where graphics as well as colour are used to assist orientation – research has proved that men, far more than women, are prone to colour-blindness. The fit-out works with the lightweight aesthetic of the buildings to promote a sense of transparency and connectivity. High-quality furniture, including designs by Mies van der Rohe and Alvar Aalto, complements the ambience of the interiors.

0   10   50m

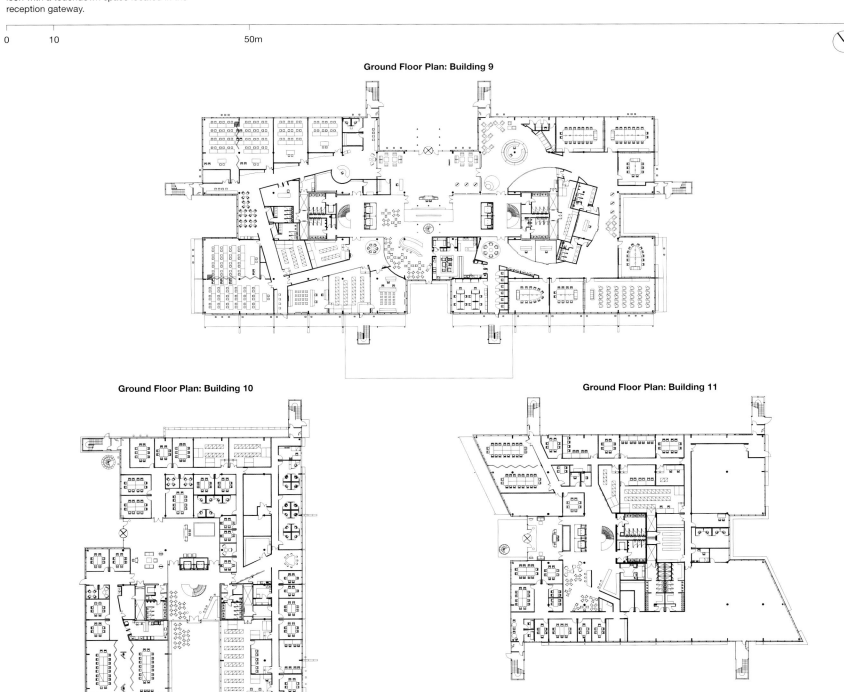

Ground Floor Plan: Building 9

Ground Floor Plan: Building 10

Ground Floor Plan: Building 11

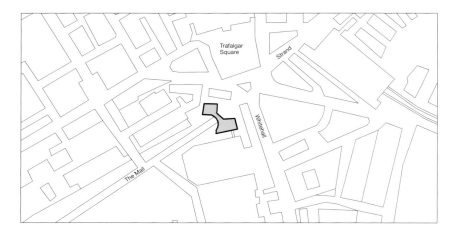

Opposite top Cleaned and restored west elevation facing The Mall.

Opposite bottom left Entrance to former First Sea Lord's residence.

Opposite bottom right By removing the lift the former lift shaft becomes a light-filled staircase.

Admiralty Arch

The Mall, Westminster
Client: Cabinet Office
Completion: 2001

Context

Admiralty Arch was completed in 1911 to designs by Sir Aston Webb, and forms the termination to the view down The Mall from Buckingham Palace. The building consists of three central arched openings, each containing massive iron gates, flanked by curved wings. It was originally occupied by the Admiralty and included a large apartment, with its own entrance, for the First Sea Lord (the leading officer of the Royal Navy). During the post-war period, it passed to the Ministry of Defence. In more recent years, the building, which contains a large quantity of office space, has had a number of uses including, briefly, a shelter for the homeless. In the late 1990s, then empty, it was ceded to the Cabinet Office along with other former Admiralty buildings on Whitehall.

Brief

When HOK was commissioned to prepare a refurbishment programme for the Arch to accommodate 400 civil servants, the building had already been cleaned and repaired externally.

The interiors, however, were in a disorganized condition, with much temporary partitioning, and services were antiquated. Once the partitioning had been stripped out, original cellular office spaces could be restored, with new open-plan offices created in the space above the arches.

Solution

New heating and ventilation ducts were inserted into wall spaces, with plant tucked away invisibly at roof level. Cabling for IT was concealed in new channels cut into the floors. Original features – including sash windows, floor surfaces and the glazed tiles used to clad corridors and stairs – were overhauled and cleaned. The entire programme of work was finished in just over a year, and marked the first completed phase of HOK's Cabinet Office project.

HOK's task at Admiralty Arch was to rediscover the original building's quality and to strip away the accretions of time and the damage done by neglect,

so that its simple, robust Edwardian architecture could be revealed. David King and Jonathan Howe, who led HOK's team, take pride in the fact that their design work was in service to the aims of the original architect, and that the success of their intervention lies in the fact that the dignified utility of the building is once more apparent to staff and visitors alike.

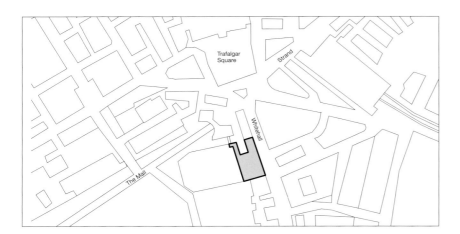

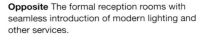

Opposite The formal reception rooms with seamless introduction of modern lighting and other services.

Admiralty House

Whitehall, Westminster
Client: Cabinet Office
Completion: 2002

Context

As part of the redevelopment of the former Admiralty buildings on Whitehall, HOK also undertook the refurbishment of Admiralty House, the former home of the First Lord of the Admiralty, completed in 1788 by Samuel Pepys Cockerell to an earlier design of Sir Robert Taylor. After a century of use it was considered too small and a new home for the First Lord was planned in Admiralty Arch, but it was never used. Winston Churchill moved his family into Admiralty House when invited to join Chamberlain's War Cabinet. In the 1960s, when Downing Street was substantially rebuilt, Admiralty House provided a temporary home and offices for prime minister Harold Macmillan and his staff.

Admiralty House is unusual in having no main entrance of its own, being reached through a lobby carved out of the south wing of the adjacent Ripley Building. The upper levels now contain private apartments for government ministers and the ground floor houses a series of formal rooms for dinners and government hospitality. These are accessed via a niched lobby and an impressive inner entrance hall with a fine staircase to the upper floor.

Brief

As with the other buildings in Whitehall, many rooms in Admiralty House are a repository of architectural salvage from earlier demolished buildings. Being confronted with such a mixture of styles challenges any architect to act with sensitivity and discretion, and it reveals HOK's ability to recognize, understand and enhance the work of previous generations. In contrast to HOK's work on other buildings in this complex, where there was a need to create modern workspaces and conserve the historic fabric, here the emphasis was on restoration.

Solution

The completed refurbishment of Admiralty House shows the respect that the HOK team had for the original architect and the recognition that a fertile architectural dialogue can occur between different generations of designers. The result is a set of elegant formal rooms that convey the era of their creation, yet benefit from the advantages of today's technology.

In Between Admiralty House and Whitehall, the former kitchens of Admiralty House currently stand disused. During the Second World War, the kitchen block was converted to a cinema using seats, lighting and projectors removed from a cinema in Kent. Here, Churchill, the chiefs of staff and guests watched films of military operations, and occasionally relaxed over a feature film. It is hard to believe that thousands of people walked by this 'most secret' room every day without the slightest suspicion of what was going on. The cinema remains (minus the Gaumont projectors, which are now in the collections of the Imperial War Museum) and there are discussions about the potential for reusing the building as a press centre, a purpose to which it would be well suited.

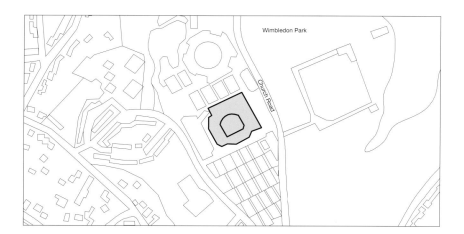

Wimbledon Park

Church Road

Opposite Premium balcony space was enhanced and extended over the main clubhouse entrance.

All England Lawn Tennis Club Members' Clubhouse

Wimbledon, Merton
Client: All England Lawn Tennis and Croquet Club
Completion: 2002

Context

Wimbledon is the global shrine of lawn tennis, but until recently its facilities – both for players and for spectators – were modest. The completion of the Millennium Building, housing new changing rooms and player facilities, allowed the All England Lawn Tennis Club (AELTC), which hosts the championships, to provide vastly improved changing rooms and other facilities for players.

Brief

As a consequence of the Millennium Building works, former changing-room spaces adjacent to Centre Court became redundant. The opportunity thus arose to create a new Clubhouse containing office, conference, function and catering spaces as well as much-improved amenities for members of the AELTC, an exclusive body which prides itself on its continuing club identity.

Solution

The overall refashioning of spaces around the Centre Court – including,
more recently, the demolition of an undistinguished 1970s extension – was undertaken by HOK Sport, and has transformed the spectators' experience of Wimbledon. HOK was commissioned to fit out the Clubhouse, rationalizing what had been a warren of rooms and providing new lounges and other hospitality spaces within the existing structure. Low ceiling heights had to be addressed – the club spaces sit below and around the terraces and Royal Box, itself refurbished and given an improved access route. In the foyer, a double-height entrance area has been created: a place where trophies – housed in magnificent, highly secure display cases act as a focus for the space, and where portraits can be displayed. The client wanted a look to the interiors that was 'traditional but with a contemporary touch'. Furnishings reflect this brief, with European oaks used extensively for fine parquet flooring and panelling. A sophisticated lighting system animates the interiors. There is a significant element of flexibility to
the fit-out, with the use of movable partitions – for example, to provide the new route to the Royal Box on those occasions, during the Championships, when it is needed.

The route taken by the players through the Clubhouse foyer was carefully considered in order to add to the sense of occasion. Every player passes the trophy cabinet and honours boards, recording past winners, before stepping into the Centre Court. A sandblasted, etched, glazed screen features players – in the dress of the 1930s, 1950s and the present day – in three phases of a service. This is a further reflection of the sense of history and tradition that pervades Wimbledon and an apt example of the way in which Andrew Warner-Lacey, the project designer, uses details to reinforce the principal theme of the design.

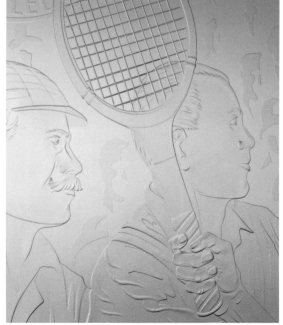

Opposite top The terrace outside the members' lounge provides dramatic views of the courts.

Opposite bottom left A double stair leads up to the members' lounge past the Championships honours boards.

Opposite bottom middle Etched glass panels and doors provide a screen between the lobby and the Centre Court.

Opposite bottom right A number of two-metre (six-foot) high display cabinets house the Championship trophies.

First Floor Plan

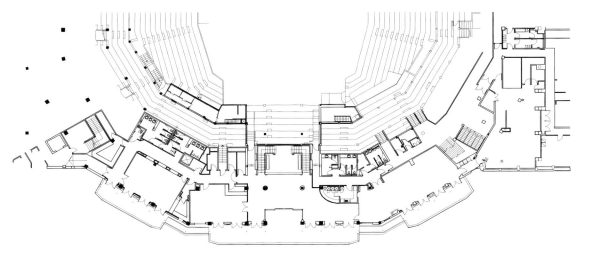

Ground Floor Plan

Section

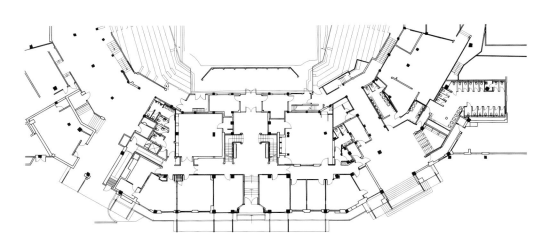

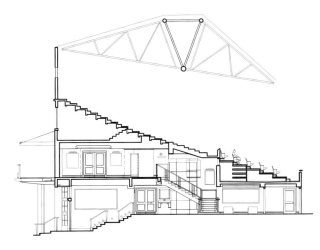

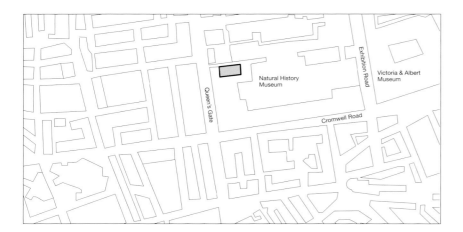

Darwin Centre, Phase One

**Natural History Museum, Cromwell Road, Kensington and Chelsea
Client: Natural History Museum
Completion: 2002**

Context
The Natural History Museum's Darwin Centre, Phase One, was a landmark project for HOK in London – one that reflects significant themes in the work of the office. It responded to a highly demanding practical and technical brief but was also a celebration of the huge body of research carried out by the Museum, of which the public is, or has been until recently, largely unaware. In fact, more than 300 scientific researchers work there.

The Natural History Museum is a repository for millions of zoological specimens stored in spirit-filled glass vessels. They include items collected by, amongst others, Captain Cook and Charles Darwin – in some cases of now-extinct species. The collection continues to grow and is ever more important as the world's biodiversity is threatened by climate change and development. Located to the west of the main museum building, the utilitarian inter-war structure that housed both collection and scientists

was essentially a warehouse. It lacked modern services (including, critically, cooling) and was disconnected from the rest of the Grade I listed Alfred Waterhouse Museum, whose director was anxious to raise public awareness of the collection, while providing secure accommodation for the scientists.

Brief
The £21 million centre housing this unique collection is a highly rational, straightforward building, driven by a functional agenda but with a sense of style and place. Building in proximity to Waterhouse was a challenge in itself, demanding protracted negotiations with English Heritage, who were anxious that there should be a clear visual relationship between old and new. The use of terracotta as a visual 'frame' for the new building façades was one obvious approach: English Heritage was particularly concerned about the western elevation on to Queen's Gate, which consequently assumed a more solid look than the architects had intended. Both English

Heritage and local planners were also concerned about the height and bulk of the building, posing a challenge to the architects in accommodating the necessary space on the site.

Solution
In 'diagram', the new HOK-designed facility is very simple. To the north, the collection is contained within a solid, heavily serviced cold store, eight storeys high. Service ducts are placed externally, so that maintenance staff do not generally need to enter the storage areas. To the south, the laboratories are placed behind a glazed elevation – an 'intelligent skin' with shading louvres that track the sun, sandwiched between two layers of glass. The double skin acts as a chimney, naturally exhausting warm air as part of a low-energy services strategy developed with engineers Buro Happold. Store and laboratories are separated by a full-height, top-lit atrium, roofed with lightweight Teflon cushions – a buffer zone, which is also the point of public access to the building. (It is additionally designed to act as a

Opposite Interior of the atrium showing the connecting bridges between laboratories and storage areas.

Bottom right The west elevation emphasizes the building diagram illustrating the storage to the north and laboratories to the south.

smoke reservoir in the event of fire.) Occupied 'bridges' containing libraries and break-out spaces span the atrium. Walkways along its southern edge allow the public, taken on conducted tours, to look into the laboratories, which have more private 'write-up' areas along the southern façade. Initially, some of the scientists were unhappy about their work being open to view and blinds are provided for privacy – in fact, however, they are virtually never pulled down, and the researchers have warmed to public interest in their work.

Simple and direct in concept, the building is carefully detailed. Enormous trouble was taken, for example, with the specification of the terracotta – the manufacturers were asked to provide panels with the slight variations of texture and colour that give the material its special qualities. The south façade, designed in association with Arup, features 104 specially made brackets of cast alloy steel, from which the glazing is hung – they are consciously zoomorphic in form though essentially practical in purpose. Here is a new approach to the decorative tradition which Waterhouse, that most practical of Victorian architects, embodied in the Natural History Museum – arguably his masterpiece. Despite its decorative façades, the original Museum is actually a highly progressive building, which made maximum use of iron and glass to provide spectacular interiors on a highly rational plan, in tune with the scientific thinking of the nineteenth century. Waterhouse was certainly an inspiration for HOK's work at the Museum, which could be seen as a continuation of his rational approach. It certainly contrasts with the more overt form-making of Daniel Libeskind's proposals for the 'Spiral' at the nearby Victoria and Albert Museum. The Darwin Centre exemplifies the way in which HOK works with tradition and context, but reinterprets both. Equally, it is a building that has transformed working practices at the Museum and provided a link between its public face and its less well-known, but equally significant, research activities.

Proceding pages The north elevation with the mechanical equipment external to the storage areas.

Opposite Typical storage area with reused timber shelving.

Below Bespoke stainless steel units made for storing large specimens.

Opposite Detail of south façade showing the terracotta finial of the gardener's cottage in the foreground and the ventilated solar cavity wall in the background.

Site Plan

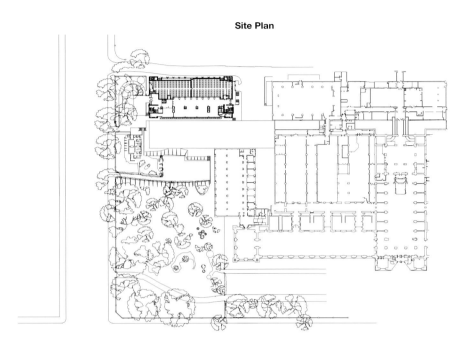

0   10   50m

Section   **South Elevation**

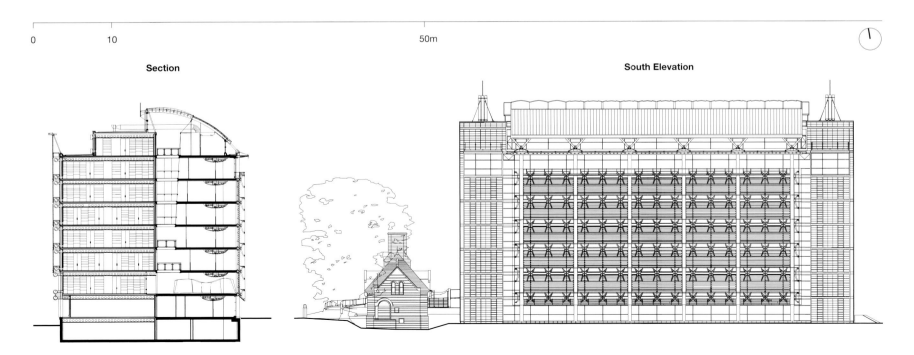

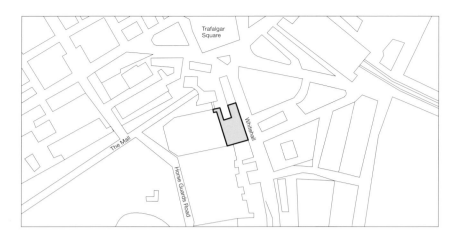

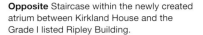
22–26 Whitehall – Cabinet Office

Whitehall, Westminster
Client: Cabinet Office
Completion: 2003

Context

The complex of buildings at 20–26 Whitehall, refurbished and adapted by HOK to house the 800-strong staff of the Cabinet Office (and, for a time, the Office of the Deputy Prime Minister), includes the Grade I listed Ripley Building (designed for the Admiralty by Thomas Ripley and completed in 1726), the famous screen of columns to Whitehall by Robert Adam (erected 1760–1), Kirkland House (a neo-Georgian building of 1929–30, unlisted and formerly housing a bank at street level with government office above) and Aston Webb's magnificent Admiralty Arch (built in 1908-11 as part of the national monument to Queen Victoria).

Brief

The HOK project was part of an ambitious programme of relocation and redevelopment of government buildings in and around Whitehall, which included the radical reconstruction of the Treasury buildings on Parliament Square where the Cabinet Office had vacated space. The buildings forming the Cabinet

Office's new home had been mostly occupied by the Ministry of Defence in the post-war period and were in a shabby state – with the Ripley Building in poor structural condition, on account of the failure of its original foundations, and requiring urgent remedial work. The project also embraced the refurbishment of S. P. Cockerell's Admiralty House as well as Admiralty Arch (see pages 102–5).

Solution

The underpinning of the Ripley Building formed a preliminary phase of the project. Its structural problems resolved, the building was the subject of a careful restoration programme undertaken in consultation with English Heritage, the Commission for Architecture and the Built Environment (CABE) and Westminster Council. The building contains some exceptional interiors that could not be altered, including the entrance hall; the boardroom, with its carved ornament attributed to Grinling Gibbons; and the former Captains' Payroom, where Nelson's body lay before his funeral

at St Paul's Cathedral. In fact, few visible changes were made in the Ripley Building, though its services were comprehensively updated. A new first-floor landing on the main stair was designed to seamlessly match the old work. In contrast, a new lift inserted into a lightwell, with the approval of English Heritage, was left exposed behind a glazed partition, introducing daylight into a dark corridor. The Ripley Building provides a series of cellular private offices and meeting rooms, while open-plan offices are contained within Kirkland House, where there was scope for radical change.

The whole complex is entered via a new reception area in Kirkland House, the former banking hall having been stripped out. A lightwell between Kirkland House and the Ripley Building, formerly a depressing dank space, was transformed into a glazed atrium which houses lifts and service risers, minimizing changes to the adjacent historic building fabric. Adjacent Georgian brick façades were repaired

and cleaned, contrasting vividly with the elegant steel-and-glass aesthetic of the new interventions. The south elevation of Kirkland House was rebuilt, so that new open-plan office floors open on to the light-filled atrium.

The complexity of the project, involving as it did conservation, restoration, adaptive reuse of space and new building – in some cases threaded into the historic fabric – required unusual care and diligence, as well as sensitivity to the needs of the existing building and future occupants. The HOK team, led by Jonathan Howe, provided the constant care and attention to detail that was required. They satisfied the stringent conditions imposed by the historic building fabric, but maintained a clear design vision focused on creating a contemporary working environment for some of Whitehall's leading civil servants.

English Heritage included the project in its publication Capital Solutions as a model of the way in which historic buildings can be adapted to meet modern needs, commenting that 'the flexible, modern office space that results is a model of clarity, transparency and minimalism, yet respects the grandeur of the historic buildings alongside'.

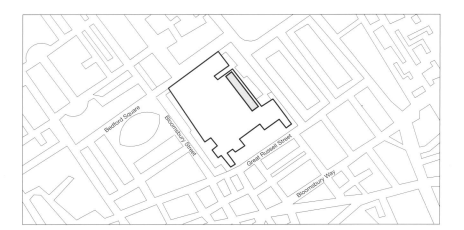

King's Library at the British Museum

Great Russell Street, Camden
Client: The British Museum
Completion: 2003

Context

The King's Library, which extends for 90 metres (300 feet) along the east side of the Great Court at the heart of the British Museum, is unquestionably one of the great interiors of London, a vision of neoclassical magnificence. It was the first part of the new museum, designed by Sir Robert Smirke, to be constructed (in 1823–7) and was built to house the great library (containing 80,000 volumes) of George III, donated to the nation by George IV and today forming part of the collections of the British Library.

In 1998 the British Library moved from Bloomsbury into its new home at St Pancras designed by Colin St John Wilson. Both the famous round Reading Room and the King's Library, minus its books, were passed back to the British Museum. The King's Library had been used by the British Library as a space for exhibitions, an inappropriate role which had meant that its historic interior was usually cluttered with temporary displays. For most visitors, it was a place of passage rather than one in which to linger.

Brief

The Museum's decision to use the King's Library as a gallery of the Enlightenment – the great movement in thought that generated the idea of the modern museum – and as an introduction to its collections as a whole provided an ideal use for this splendid room. The £7 million project – an accompaniment to the re-roofing of the Great Court by Foster & Partners – had to be completed in time for opening in 2003, the 250th anniversary of the foundation of the British Museum as the world's first national public museum. The essence of the client brief was that 'the room itself should be the first exhibit'. Its architecture and decor should be not only respected, but enhanced.

Solution

For HOK's conservation and cultural heritage group, led by Neil Cooke, the starting point for the project was the conducting of detailed research into the fabric and its history, which would feed into the work of the design team led by Simon Douch. Although little-altered (unlike most of the Museum's interior) the King's Library was in a shabby condition, with its original decorative scheme obscured. There was concern about the state of the ceiling, after bomb damage in 1940, and extensive repairs to the plaster were carried out prior to the reinstatement of the authentic colour scheme, with specialist advisors supplementing HOK's own expertise. The oak floorboards were also carefully repaired – they had never been lifted since the floor was laid in 1827. Marble surrounds and scagliola pilasters were cleaned and restored. Given the Library's Grade I listing, regular consultation with English Heritage was mandatory – producing an amicable collaboration.

Crucially, the services within the room needed to be greatly upgraded to equip it for its new use. A modern cooling system was required and the historic book presses (206 in total), which had

been fitted with glazing in the 1850s, had to be equipped with lighting and security systems so that they could be used to house material from the Museum's collections and items on loan from other institutions. In the completed ensemble around 3,000 artefacts are on show, with the remaining spaces in the presses filled with books from the Museum's own collections and the House of Commons Library. Voids below the floor, supported on brick jack arches and used for heating, were utilized to contain ventilation ducts, with additional floor grilles modelled on surviving originals. Fibre-optic lighting was used to illuminate the presses; a major advantage being that it does not generate heat. Voids discovered behind the presses provided access routes for cabling. In addition to the book presses, six original floor-mounted display cases survived. These were restored and additional replicas were made, with cabling provided from below.

As part of the project, the Long Room, east of the King's Library, which had

been constructed as a book store in the 1840s and latterly partitioned into offices, was restored and refurbished to house support spaces for events held in the Library, accommodation for the Museum's Friends and a reading room for its own library and archives.

The King's Library is a celebration of the idea of the museum, and a place where an extraordinary range of objects – some beautiful, others curious – can be studied and enjoyed in an exhilarating setting. It is a place for discovering and for understanding the connections between the various collections that the Museum itself contains, as well as the connections between it and other institutions – for example, the Natural History Museum was once part of the British Museum. With busts and antique vases displayed on pedestals, the King's Library has the ambience of a great library of the Enlightenment, though in this case not the private preserve of a monarch or scholarly aristocrat, but one that is open to all.

0   10   50m

Ceiling Plan

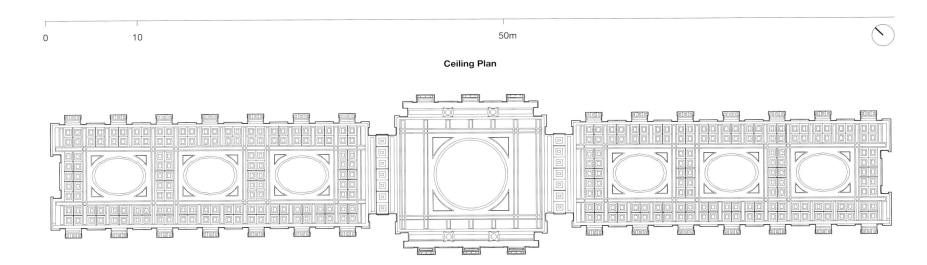

Floor Plan

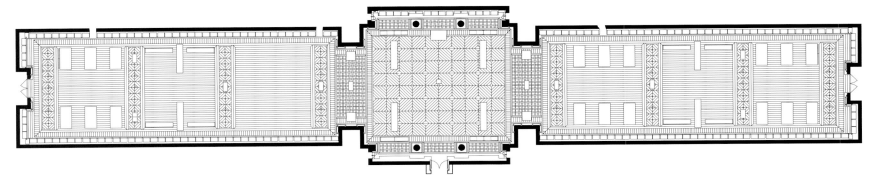

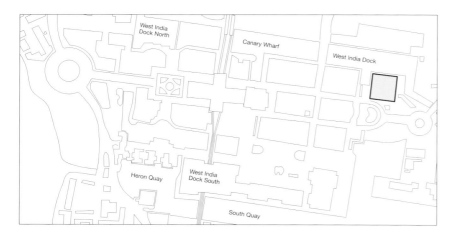

Barclays Bank Headquarters

One Churchill Place, Canary Wharf, Tower Hamlets
Client: Canary Wharf Contractors Ltd
Completion: 2004

Context

Although today a global provider of financial services, Barclays is an old City of London institution, with its origins in the reign of Charles II. Its move to Canary Wharf in 2005 was therefore a landmark event, even for a development that is now home to many leading finance operations. These include Barclays' rival, HSBC, housed in a Foster-designed tower just west of the 32-storey HOK-designed Barclays Bank Headquarters.

Brief

HOK won the project in competition with SOM and Cesar Pelli and Associates, both practices with a long association with Canary Wharf – SOM's 1980s masterplan is still the template for development there. Barclays was planning to vacate a series of buildings in the City, including its prominent headquarters block on Lombard Street. The brief was for a building of around 93,000 square metres (1 million square feet), capable of accommodating more than 6,000 members of staff in largely open-plan office space, together with some cellular office space for senior staff. (Currently, Barclays occupies around two-thirds of the space, with the remainder let.) Dealing floors were not required, since Barclays' dealing operations are housed elsewhere at Canary Wharf. The bank saw the move as the opportunity for a 'culture change', with the new building encouraging more interaction between staff who had hitherto been scattered across a series of locations. The client wanted a building that expressed openness and efficiency, with less of the extraneous display seen in some of the earlier blocks at 'the Wharf'.

Solution

Entering the ground-floor lobby – light, clean and with a conspicuous absence of heavy decor – the visitor immediately senses that this is a building with a distinctive personality. The use of colourful and figured marbles – a feature of many other Canary Wharf developments – is restricted to the lift lobbies beyond. However, Barclays is also a building that extends the 'vocabulary' of Canary Wharf in other ways. Since the inception of the development, central service cores have been de rigueur in the office buildings there, in line with standard American practice – even Norman Foster, whose tower in Hong Kong for HSBC was highly innovative in its day, was obliged to fall in line here. With the overall profile of the building – height and volume – set by the masterplan, HOK proposed a departure from standard practice. They concentrated devolved service cores to the north of the site and designed a series of (mostly) six-storey glazed atria extending up the southern face of the building, which could be working spaces as well as places to relax over a coffee. These atria are fundamental to the project and are airy, light-filled spaces, which are heavily used. At most times of the day it is usual to find two or three colleagues having an informal working meeting, or an individual quietly tapping away at a laptop as others take a break from

Opposite The south elevation, illustrating the stacked atria.

Below Barclays to the far right in Canary Wharf.

Right Detail of the south curtain wall and entrance canopy

their desks. Each atrium has a visual theme: one has a grove of thriving bamboos, for example, with a hanging sculpture that continues the theme. The views from offices into the atria are a feature of a building in which visual connectivity is a guiding principle.

Externally, the atria can be clearly seen rising up the south face of the tower, the strong and individual identity of which is reinforced by the façade treatment. Depending on the time of day and the light conditions, the building reads variously as an all-glass structure or as one where the stainless-steel mullions of the glazing emerge to give it a very different, more solid, character. Avoiding complex glazing solutions, the architects went for a very straightforward system in which the façade is hung from a series of great steel masts, perhaps consciously nautical in flavour, which rise the height of the tower through the atria. The special sparkle in the stainless steel is the outcome of studies that established that giving the steel a stippled 'linen'

texture provided maximum reflectivity, even on dull days.

Work began on site in November 2001 (the project was completed to base build just under two years later, with fit-out completed during 2005). With the attack on New York's World Trade Center a very recent memory, the structure of the tower was designed to address a variety of emergency conditions. In addition, the internal stair cores can contain the entire population of the building using a strategy of 'invacuation' – innovative at the time, but since copied in many new designs. The cantilevered corners of the tower provide attractive meeting spaces on all floors, and reduce the overall steel load. Floors are typically of around 3,200 square metres (34,000 square feet), with some extending to 3,500 square metres (38,000 square feet) where they do not embrace atria. Below street level, the base of the building provides connections to the retail centre and to Canary Wharf Underground Station, heavily used

by Barclays' staff – parking on site is minimal. There is also a fitness centre at this level.

Canary Wharf has not been always been regarded as an innovator in energy and environmental issues. At Barclays, the banks of atria, which act as an energy buffer, plus a 'green' roof – the first in the Isle of Dogs and claimed, at 160 metres (520 feet) above street level, as the highest in Europe – are elements in an environmental strategy that won a BREEAM rating of 'excellent' and a series of sustainability awards. No other building at Canary Wharf to date has achieved such recognition – another way in which HOK has broken the mould.

This is a classic HOK London project. HOK's design director, Larry Malcic, believes that it is 'a good example of the way in which we explore the potential for reinventing a building type – Barclays is highly innovative, both in concept and execution, but it wears its innovative aspects lightly'.

Malcic worked closely with senior designers Christopher Colosimo and Chris Yoon to create a highly efficient, well-crafted and classically elegant tower. Supporting the design effort was a large team led by David King, Rich Drozd and Phong Tran, who were able to deliver the promise of the design idea with record speed – Bob Phelan, from Canary Wharf, explained, 'We usually "Fast Track" projects, but Barclays was "Turbo Track" delivery.' Barclays is one of the new stars of Docklands – no wonder that HOK is currently completing another building on an adjacent site.

Left Detail of the base of the building, showing the reflective quality of the glass and stainless steel.

Opposite A typical six-storey atrium with a simple mast structure supporting the double-height glazing.

Left The main lobby uses French limestone and translucent glass, which provides a refreshing lightness.

Right The uppermost atrium, with its glass roof modulated by translucent fabric 'clouds'.

Bottom right Detail of the lower-level entrance.

Opposite The Barclays tower viewed from the east with the stainless steel cladding reflecting the sun.

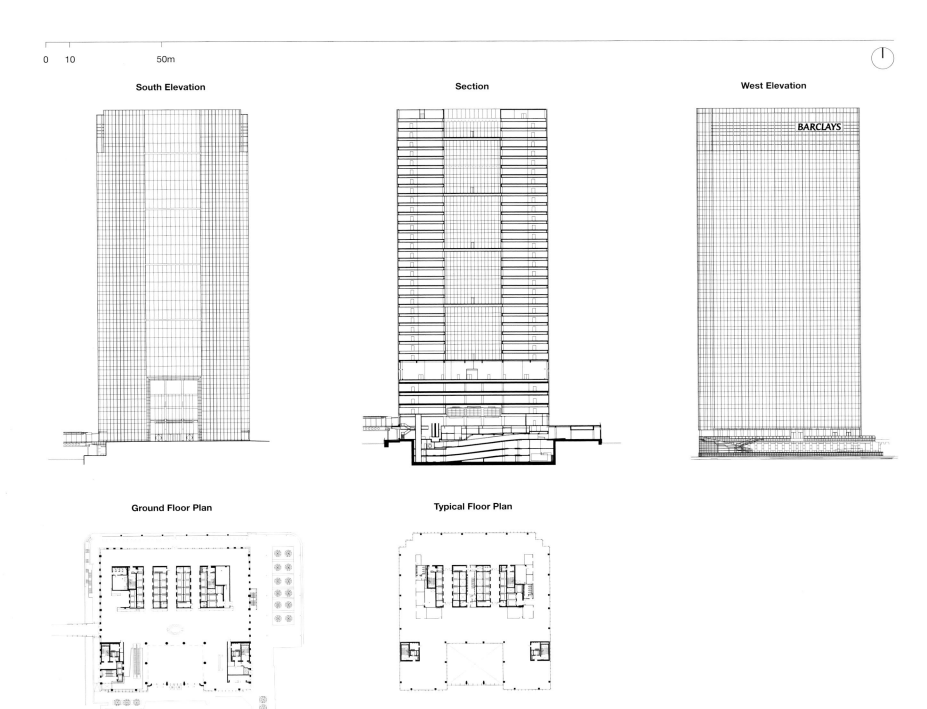

0   10   50m

South Elevation

Section

West Elevation

BARCLAYS

Ground Floor Plan

Typical Floor Plan

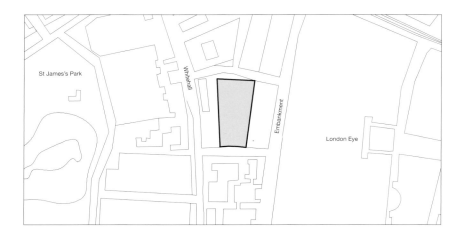

St James's Park
Whitehall
Embankment
London Eye

Ministry of Defence – Main Building

Whitehall, Westminster
Client: Ministry of Defence
Completion: 2004

Context

The formidable architectural historian Nikolaus Pevsner described the massive Ministry of Defence (MoD) building on Whitehall as 'a monument of tiredness', deplorably out-of-tune, in his view, with the progressive architectural scene in Britain after the Second World War. In fact, the project dated back to the years before the First World War and to an architectural competition for a new government building, initially planned to house the Board of Trade, held in 1913 and won two years later by the youthful Emmanuel Vincent Harris (who was serving in the trenches when he heard of his success). Because of the war, the project was held in abeyance, and construction began only in 1938 – to an enlarged design – only to be halted by the outbreak of a second great European conflict. The entire complex, 170 metres (560 feet) long and eight storeys high, was completed as late as 1959, by which time it seemed hopelessly out-of-date to progressive critics like Pevsner.

More recently, its merits have been more objectively considered and the building is now Grade I listed. The listing is, however, due in no small part to the incorporation within Harris's building of a vaulted wine-cellar that dates from c.1530, which was once part of Whitehall Palace and is now a scheduled ancient monument. There are also a number of fine period rooms salvaged from buildings (Pembroke House and Cromwell House) that were demolished in the 1930s to make way for the new ministry.

The greater part of the interior of Harris's building consisted of cellular offices arranged along central corridors. The finest of the interiors – the preserved historic rooms apart – were at ground level, where an impressive pillared hall, a good example of 'stripped Classicism', formed the central focus of an axis extending the length of the building. In recent years, extraordinarily, this fine space had degenerated into use as a furniture store.

Brief

HOK's involvement with the MoD began in 1998. The ministry had carried out a review of its central London estate and concluded that it had too many buildings, including several converted hotels, generating high running costs, with staff inconveniently divided between them. In addition, its main building in Whitehall, where 2,600 staff were based, was in need of major refurbishment to meet more stringent health and safety standards. It was decided that Harris's building should be upgraded to meet these standards and that there was scope for it to provide space for around 700 more staff. In line with practice in the commercial sector, the bulk of the space in the building was to be converted from cellular to open-plan offices. The £352 million reconstruction project, intended to streamline the operations of the MoD, was to be undertaken under a PFI contract, in line with government policy. In 2000, the Modus consortium was awarded the contract and HOK was appointed architect as part of a

Opposite The pillared hall – formerly part of a ceremonial route – has become the new heart of the building.

Right View of the building designed in 1913 and completed in 1959, as seen from the South Bank.

multi-disciplinary team. The radical nature of the reconstruction involved decanting staff to other buildings in the area, most of which have since been relinquished by the MoD, with the exception of the Old War Office which had been comprehensively refurbished in 1985–92.

The appointment of HOK followed on from the practice's long-standing involvement with a number of government buildings in Whitehall (see pages 58–67 and 120–4). However, the MoD project drew on major strengths that no comparable commercial practice could muster: expertise in the conservation of historic buildings and experience at reworking existing buildings to accommodate new approaches to workplace design. The technical brief was further complicated by the need to incorporate sophisticated security measures.

Solution
Harris's building is wedge-shaped, with two long wings of accommodation to

east and west linked by cross wings and a central circulation spine which enclosed three courtyards. The cross wings now contain support spaces, including WCs, IT spaces, meeting rooms and coffee points. Only nine cellular offices were retained in the entire building – a reflection of the MoD's determination to end the inefficient use of space, perpetuated for too long by outdated hierarchies. The rationale of the transformation was to create workspaces that encouraged greater communication and interaction between staff (both civil servants and services personnel).

The ground floor of the building was reconfigured as a series of communal spaces used by MoD staff and visitors. The showpiece here is the restored pillared hall, now containing a café which acts as a centre of activity, with informal meetings and encounters between staff generating the interaction that the client brief demanded. Handsome light fittings, designed in the spirit of Harris's architecture, lend a

sparkle to the space. Though security is understandably tight, this level of the building is a semi-public space – members of the press come here for briefings, for example – and its 'village' ambience is what one would expect in any large commercial headquarters. Equally, the department's civil servants now enjoy working conditions of a contemporary commercial standard, and the image of the building as a secretive fortress has, as far as possible, been dispelled. The glazing-over of the three central courtyards in the building has turned what were, in fact, rather gloomy lightwells into usable and enjoyable spaces – the main staff restaurant spills over into one of them. Another new amenity is the well-equipped 200-seat conference centre, with communication links for video and satellite conferencing.

Works to the historic rooms were essentially concerned with restoring and repairing what existed, with original colour schemes carefully researched and authentically reinstated, and

renewing lighting and other services. The services strategy for the building, developed by WSP, involved the use of chilled beams, offering real benefits in running costs over conventional cooling systems. The installation of a combined heat and power generator further reduced both costs and carbon emissions and helped to gain the building a 'very good' BREEAM rating. As part of the project, issues of accessibility were addressed throughout the building.

The project reflected government determination to bring its own operations into line with those of the private sector and to use its estate effectively. HOK's experience in designing workplaces was vital to its success: the organizational elements of the project were fundamental, but the way in which the qualities of a long-undervalued building have been revealed is equally impressive. Ian Fleetwood, senior designer, showed that flair and creativity are fundamental requirements for a major refurbishment.

Opposite One of the bed chambers from Pembroke House, designed by Sir William Chambers, relocated from buildings demolished in the 1930s.

Right Typical open-plan office space created from former cellular offices.

Bottom right Lobby space around the new conference suite.

Preceding pages Glazed extension to the staff restaurant within one of the atria.

Opposite Atrium seating area.

Below South entrance lobby – a fine example of 'stripped classicism'.

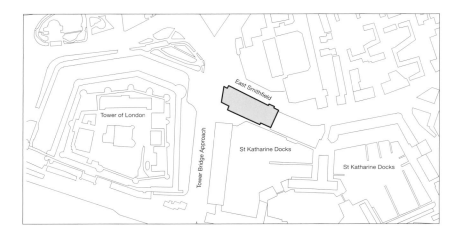

Tower of London

East Smithfield

Tower Bridge Approach

St Katharine Docks

St Katharine Docks

Reynolds Porter Chamberlain

St Katharine's Way, St Katharine Docks, Tower Hamlets
Client: Reynolds Porter Chamberlain
Completion: 2006

Context
Reynolds Porter Chamberlain's (RPC's) aspiration is to 'be seen as London's most pragmatic, open and collaborative law firm' with an 'open, accessible and transparent way of doing business'. This ethos was reflected in the company's brief to HOK for the fit-out of nearly 9,000 square metres (95,000 square feet) of space (over four floor levels) in a recently completed Rogers Stirk Harbour & Partners building close to Tower Bridge in the City of London. This is a dramatic structure, with a central atrium and bridges connecting floors across the void. The law firm had nearly 500 staff and was planning for further growth. The move coincided with a re-branding exercise, and the colour scheme in the new offices reflected the new brand identity.

Brief
The client's decision to opt for an open-plan work style was radical for the law business, but RPC, which works largely in the insurance sector, wanted a high degree of flexibility, allowing it to relocate staff easily and move and reassemble teams as its operations demanded. It felt that traditional hierarchies needed to be challenged. The colourful and light-filled interior projects an image of the legal profession far removed from most people's preconceptions.

Solution
The views across the dock were a considerable attraction of the location, and HOK have maximized the view for both staff and visitors alike. The conference suite, directly behind the reception, occupies the central zone of the building with back-to-back meeting rooms. This has freed the rooms from the glazed perimeter and opened up the view to all. Wanting to provide the best views to users of the meeting rooms, RPC's all-important legal seminars were intended to take place in the training suite, comprising large meeting rooms with flexible partitioning. The business lounge, where the post-seminar refreshments are served, also has a view of the dock and doubles up as a break-out space for clients trapped in long meetings.

In the interests of the lawyers, who had bravely committed to an open-plan environment, the reduction of potentially disturbing noise was critical. At each entry point – there are two per floor – all of the ancillary facilities are behind a screen and well out of earshot of the workforce. Coat cupboards, tea and water points, pigeon-holes, lockers, recycling, copying, scanning and printing are in a dense, but carefully thought-out sequence of spaces. Reprographic facilities are also concealed from the office areas at each end of the office.

RPC offloaded 3.5 kilometres (2.2 miles) of filing before the move – equivalent to the distance from their old office to their new! Minimal personal filing is provided in the new premises, and a degree of local filing is available in low-level cabinets. The majority of it is now managed centrally in electrically-operated roller racking. This has allowed the paper-free-desk policy to actually become an achievable reality and not just a management pipe-dream.

0   10   50m

First Floor Plan

Third Floor Plan

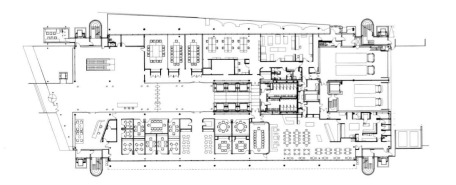

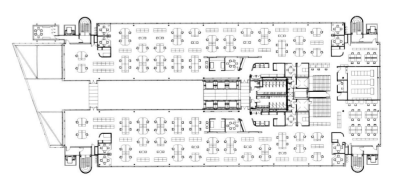

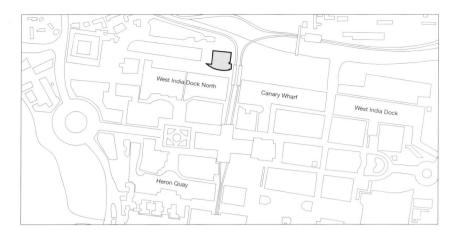

Opposite The prow of the glass and stainless steel tower contrasts with the panelized terracotta of the podium.

West India Quay Tower

Hertsmere Road, West India Quay, Tower Hamlets
Client: West India Quay Development Corporation Ltd (joint venture with MWB and Manhattan Lofts)
Completion: 2004

Context
Across the dock from the centre of Canary Wharf – with its high-rise office buildings, including HOK's headquarters for Barclays Bank – West India Quay preserves the most important run of surviving Georgian warehouses in London. Long empty, these fine late-eighteenth-century structures have now been converted into apartments, with bars and restaurants at quay level (where massive cranes have been retained, animating the space more effectively than most pieces of public art). A bridge designed by Future Systems provides a link to the offices across the water.

Brief
When HOK was commissioned to work on this project, the client had an existing planning consent for the site, so that the mix of uses was already established. The West India Quay tower scheme as developed by the architects is an undeniably bold intervention into the historic context.

Solution
At 32 storeys, HOK's residential tower is overtopped by some of the adjacent office buildings, but remains a striking exemplar of the possibilities of high-rise living in London. The first 12 storeys of the tower house a 300-key Marriott hotel, with 154 apartments and six penthouses above. The restaurants, bars, banqueting and public spaces of the hotel are housed in a lower podium block, entered from the north and clad in terracotta panels – the earthen material providing a visual connection to the stock brick of the warehouses.

Above, the tower – containing the bulk of the guest rooms for the hotel – is clad in a sheer, fastidiously detailed skin of metal and glass, with stainless-steel ribs providing a horizontal balance to the verticality of the tower and a visual link to the adjacent warehouses. The use of high-performance glass, with opening windows, counteracts solar gain on the south-facing façade. The glazing system is also designed to muffle noise from the Docklands Light Railway, which runs immediately to the east of the building.

Structurally, the building is notable as one of the first post-tensioned concrete-framed towers in London, employing a system widely used in the USA and the Far East, which reduced construction time by around 30 per cent. Thin concrete floor slabs provide generous internal floor-to-ceiling heights of 2.7 to 2.95 metres (9 to 9½ feet) while reducing the overall height of the tower.

The elegance of this building contrasts sharply with some of the more bulky Postmodernist blocks constructed in the early days of Canary Wharf. The tower comes to an acute angle on its western edge, where a sharp 'prow' contains double-height living rooms for the duplex apartments. Internally, detailing is of a high standard, and there are touches that set the interiors apart from the general run of Docklands residential developments.

Opposite The northwest corner of the tower rises dramatically over the hotel podium.

Right The slenderness of the tower is emphasized by the acute angle of the prow.

Below The deeply projecting stainless steel sills of the south-facing windows catch the afternoon light.

Opposite top Dramatic views from the
double-height living space.

Opposite bottom left Mailboxes in the lobby
become illuminated sculptural objects.

Opposite bottom right The lobby of
the Marriott hotel is designed in a
contemporary manner.

0   10   50m

Typical Floor Plans

Section

Ground Floor Plan

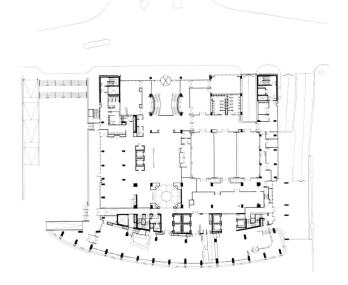

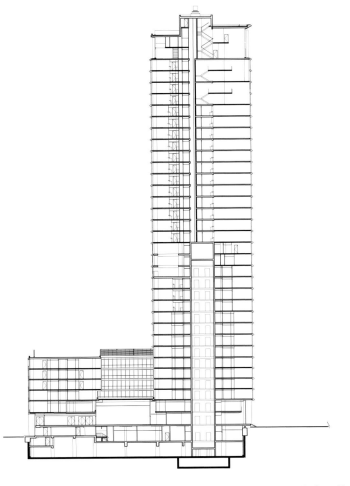

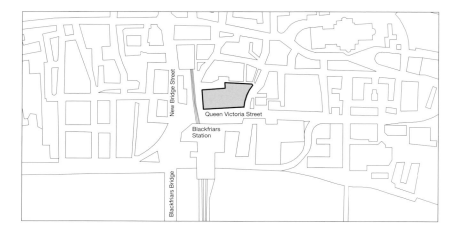

Opposite Top Identical break-out spaces on adjacent floors created a bold impression from the atrium space they overlook.

Opposite bottom left Generous corridor space within the conference suite is used for functions and is enhanced by dramatic lighting.

Opposite bottom middle The restaurant provides sustenance to lawyers working long hours.

Opposite bottom right A pivoting wall enables rooms to conjoin with the corridor to further expand the usable function space.

Dechert

Queen Victoria Street,
City of London
Client: Dechert
Completion: 2005

Context

Dechert, an Anglo-American law firm, which had been based in offices close to the Inns of Court, moved to new offices in the City of London in 2005. The 5,000 square metres (55,000 square feet) of new-build space, spread across three floors, addressed the needs of the growing company, and HOK was involved in advising on the selection of the new location and designing the fit-out of the new offices.

Brief

The project began with a very detailed analysis of Dechert's operational needs, which involved interviewing staff at all levels and workshops at which partners discussed their requirements and aspirations. Dechert's office culture, more American than British in style, demanded the retention of a high degree of cellular space, with traditional hierarchies in mind.

Solution

Two of the three floors are used for the practice of law, with cellular offices at the perimeter for lawyers, whose business involves a high degree of confidentiality, and administrative offices around a central atrium with open-plan space for administrative staff between (where sight-lines across the space are important). The third floor contains the reception and client-facing meeting facilities. In this compact environment, there is no room for spaces that cannot readily be used to aid Dechert in the business of law, so the meeting rooms are designed to be flexible. Pivoting and folding walls, and doors that hinge back to become part of the panelling, allow the rooms to be reconfigured so that they can be used for seminars and lectures, cocktail parties and other promotional events, as well as a dining suite for partners and clients. Staff dining is provided by a modern high-street-style café on the fourth floor, leading onto a terrace with views of St Paul's Cathedral.

The scheme emphasized the need for a innovative, creative and functional space that allowed for transparency and connection between working spaces, while recognizing the client's desire for a high proportion of more private spaces in line with the needs of the business. The success of the environment was largely dependent upon a design that emphasized clean lines and quality of detailing. All veneers of fiddleback sycamore, used throughout, are Forest Stewardship Council certified from sustainable sources. Careful use of feature colours and the specification of high-quality furnishings contribute to the success of the interior. The purposeful combination of design flair, sustainability and effective use of space owes much to the efforts of Colin Mulholland, senior designer for the project.

0   10   50m

Level 4 Floor Plan   **Level 5 Floor Plan**

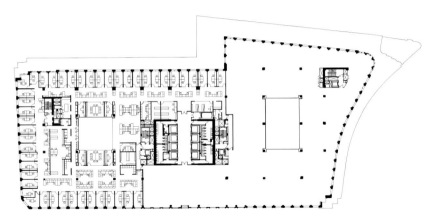

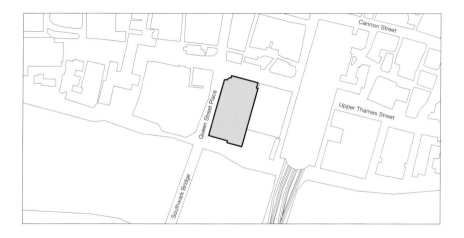

Opposite On view from the lift lobby, the library conference room displays leather-bound law books and awards, providing reassurance to visitors.

SJ Berwin

Queen Street Place, City of London
Client: SJ Berwin
Completion: 2005

Context
The law practice of SJ Berwin, employing over 1,000 staff and amongst the top ten British legal firms, was founded only in the 1980s but has become a major player on the European scene. When it approached HOK for advice on a move to new premises in 2003, its operations were spread inconveniently across three buildings in the Grays Inn Road area. The offices there were seen as tired, drab and a poor reflection on the firm's success. The expiry of the lease on the largest of them was the catalyst for relocation.

Brief
SJ Berwin saw the move as the opportunity for some radical thinking about its ways of working. The firm wanted to attract and retain the best staff and to create offices where employees and clients would feel at ease in an environment in which the old 'front office/back office' divide was abolished. The choice of a new location fell on 10 Queen Street Place (formerly

known as Thames Exchange), on the north side of Southwark Bridge. This 1980s block, with its 4,600 square metre (50,000 square foot) floorplates, had been occupied by HSBC prior to its move to Canary Wharf, and had housed dealing floors.

Solution
The bold adaptation of the building for its new user was carried out by John Robertson Architects, with a new fourth floor added. Because of the restrictions imposed by the St Paul's heights Policy, this new storey had to be cut back to the river, producing a large (2,300 square metre/25,000 square foot) rooftop garden, which is used for client receptions and staff barbecues. Internally, cellular offices – regarded as de rigueur by the client – are arranged around a new central atrium, with glass bridges and wall-climber lifts, leaving the perimeter spaces, with views over the river and of St Paul's Cathedral, as communal break-out areas with coffee points and informal seating. One of the aims was to entice the lawyers to leave

their private offices and work in the open-plan work zones. Three café/restaurant areas at ground, first and second-floor levels, provide excellent staff facilities and supersede the traditional hierarchy of private dining rooms for partners and a cafeteria for the rest. As negotiations often have to coincide with working hours in Sydney or Los Angeles, sleep pods are provided for those who have to be in the building overnight.

HOK's interior masterplan was the basis for the fit-out, designed by Andrew Warner-Lacey in association with Seth Stein Architects. Although the budget was modest and there was no desire to be showy, the public spaces are colourful and beautifully detailed. Lighting has been used to good effect throughout: the light cube in the entrance lobby is a memorable feature, housing staircases and changing colour regularly. SJ Berwin's new offices set a new standard for corporate design, which other London law firms have since taken as a benchmark.

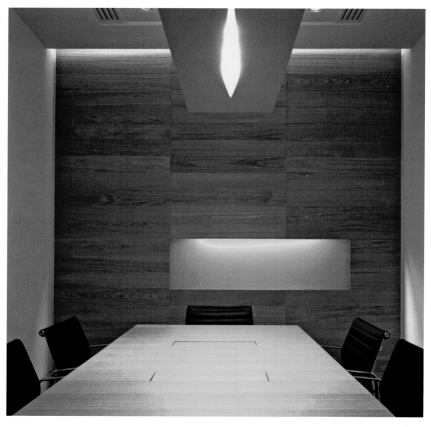

Opposite top left The general atrium coffee bar provides refreshment and access to news in a dynamic setting.

Opposite top right Steel helical staircases link floors, actively fostering staff interaction.

Opposite bottom left The client reception provides a calm waiting area away from the busy entrance.

Opposite bottom right Internal meeting rooms provide interest through careful lighting and selection of unusual material.

Right Break-out spaces located at each end of the building offer views of the river and St Paul's Cathedral.

Far right The 2,300 square metre (25,000 square foot) roof terrace provides a series of private and public spaces for staff and client entertainment.

0   10   50m

First Floor Plan

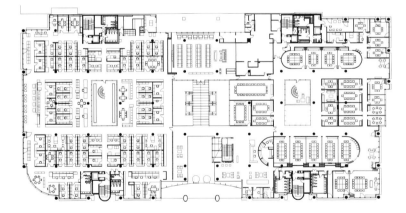

Fourth Floor Plan

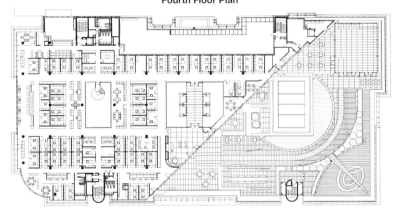

Ground Floor Plan

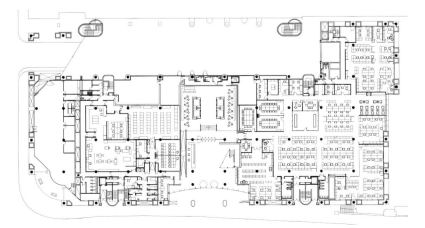

Second Floor Plan

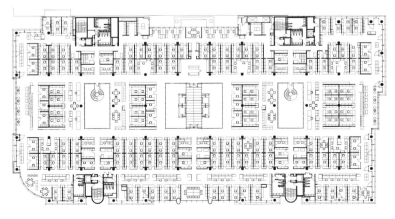

Palace of Westminster Committee Rooms

Parliament Square, Westminster
Client: Parliamentary Works
Services Directorate
Completion: 2006

Context
HOK's involvement with the Palace of Westminster dates back to 1993, when the practice was commissioned to prepare a masterplan for rationalizing and modernizing the catering facilities that serve peers, MPs, press, visitors and the more than 3,000 members of staff working in this famous Grade I listed building. The catering operations at Westminster were spread over three floors, leading to poor use of space, inefficient working practices and substandard working conditions. A six-year programme of works remedied the situation, creating new kitchen areas and refurbishing dining rooms and bars. It was based on detailed research into the fabric of the building, identifying areas where change was possible and those that were sacrosanct – in effect, all new work in the building had to blend seamlessly into the historic interiors. Both English Heritage and Westminster Council closely monitored the project.

Brief
This project provided a base of information and experience that underpinned HOK's continuing work on the Palace of Westminster. The most important element in this programme so far, commencing in 1997, has been the refurbishment of 17 House of Commons committee rooms, followed by that of several committee rooms and other spaces used by the House of Lords. These spaces are intensively used during parliamentary sessions, so that work could only take place during the long summer recess and had to be completed on schedule. Notable for their well-preserved Pugin decor, the committee rooms lacked efficient ventilation and modern fire-detection systems. Electrical wiring needed renewal, and there was a lack of provision for IT systems and broadcasting. All new services had to be accommodated without visible impact on the interiors. The Victorian panelling, furnishings and other features also needed cleaning and repair.

Solution
The new ventilation system in the committee rooms has been cleverly concealed within ceiling and floor voids, with vents incorporated into window bays. Power and data outlets and fire detectors have similarly been installed without damage to the fabric. Woodwork and ceilings were cleaned, furniture repaired and light fittings rewired. Walls have been re-covered where necessary using authentic hand-blocked papers. Window glazing has been replaced with new glass designed to resist bomb attacks.

Even as the 10-year programme of work on the committee rooms was being completed, HOK was working on a detailed survey of the entire estate of the House of Commons and looking at ways in which it could be used more efficiently in line with modern working practices.

Opposite Small House of Commons committee room with new services seamlessly woven into the original historic interior.

Below A restored committee room used by the House of Lords.

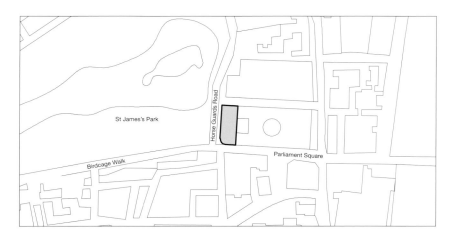

St James's Park
Horse Guards Road
Birdcage Walk
Parliament Square

Opposite Joint Chiefs of Staff conference room restored in accordance with photographs taken in 1945.

Churchill Museum and Cabinet War Rooms

King Charles Street, Westminster
Client: Imperial War Museum
Completion: 2005

Context

Located below the massive block of government offices (completed in 1915, and latterly housing the Treasury), the Churchill Museum forms an extension to the Cabinet War Rooms. Containing control and meeting rooms, a broadcasting studio, operating theatre, offices and sleeping accommodation for up to 270 people, the War Rooms were a vital part of Britain's war strategy between 1939 and 1945 – and were actually extended several times during the course of the conflict.

In 1945, they were closed and, for nearly four decades, were used largely for the storage of Treasury archives – although some key interiors were preserved. Their very existence, buried below a massive concrete raft, was kept secret. In 1984, however, part of the complex was opened to visitors by the Imperial War Museum and became a popular visitor attraction. The approach was very much to show the spaces as they were during the war – a good photographic record fortunately existed.

Brief

The idea of a museum devoted to the life and achievements of Winston Churchill, forming an extension to the War Rooms, had existed for some time. However, at the turn of the twenty-first century, additional basement space, east of the existing War Rooms and formerly used for storage, became available. This was as a result of the major PFI-funded redevelopment of the Government Offices Great George Street (GOGGS), which began in 2000.

Solution

Neil Cooke of HOK was part of the team that developed the strategy for the project, which included a detailed assessment of conservation issues. HOK was subsequently commissioned to extend the War Rooms, with the Churchill Suite and other long-secret rooms used by the prime minister and his staff opened to the public in 2003. The approach was that adopted in the earlier phase of the project – an insistence on authenticity, with rooms furnished exactly as they

would have been during the Second World War. The aim, says Cooke, who has confessed to a fascination with basements, was 'simply to ensure that the finished result captures the mood of the country during the period'. The task, he says, was 'one of maintaining rooms within their historical context – complete with dust'.

Most of the spaces were in appalling condition – in some cases deep in foul water from leaking drains. Especially complex were the issues of access, fire safety, escape routes and servicing. The project benefited from a degree of integration with the GOGGS development – chilled water for cooling, for example, being provided from the system installed in the latter. The planning strategy included provision for the new Churchill Museum, opened in 2005 to mark the 40th anniversary of Churchill's death and containing a large number of artefacts and documents relating to the great man's life. The inspired exhibition design was the work of Casson Mann.

Opposite Kitchen restored to match photographs taken in 1945.

Right Churchill's private dining room containing original furnishings.

Bottom right Central corridor after restoration.

Left and below Churchill Museum exhibition design by Casson Mann within the space created by HOK.

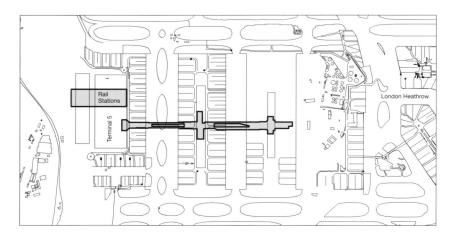

Rail Stations

London Heathrow

Terminal 5

Terminal 5 Transport Interchange

Heathrow Airport, Hillingdon, Middlesex
Client: BAA plc
Completion: 2008

Context
A competition for the design of Heathrow Airport's Terminal 5 was held in 1989 and won by Richard Rogers Partnership. Objections to the expansion of the airport led to a protracted planning inquiry and significant revisions to the original scheme, with full planning consent being obtained only in 2001. Strict constraints were placed on parking provision following the reduction of the site area, and it is envisaged that the great majority of travellers will arrive at and depart from the terminal using public transport – via the Heathrow Express, London Underground and, in the future, through-trains that could serve British provincial cities and European destinations via the Channel Tunnel.

HOK's role in the Terminal 5 project has been substantial, with a broad consultative role, drawing on the practice's extensive experience of airport design from 1995 onwards. (Its work elsewhere at Heathrow includes the Pier 5 extension and improvements

to Terminal 3.) HOK subsequently became involved in the interior architecture of the Terminal 5 building, and its 85,000 square metre (900,000 square foot) satellite – one of two planned. In 1998, it was appointed to design the rail facilities for the terminal and subsequently to work on the transit system linking terminal and satellite.

Brief
As of 2008, Heathrow Express and Underground trains will arrive at platforms 12 metres (40 feet) below ground level, constructed in what HOK director Richard Spencer describes as 'an enormous hole', 90 metres wide and 200 metres long (300 x 650 feet), excavated in front of the main terminal building. (An early idea of integrating the station within the terminal, with platforms dramatically opening to the internal space, proved impractical, particularly in terms of passenger circulation.)

The client brief for the station contained several key provisions. It was to be as far removed in character as possible

from the existing Underground stations at Heathrow – a feeling of openness, space and a clear sense of direction were vital. The station should be filled with natural light.

Solution
Accordingly, HOK set out to provide 'the best rail to air experience at any airport in the world'. The great concourse of the new building has the character of a mainline station. The use of glazing to provide fire and security compartmentation ensures that the unity of the space is retained. There is a very clear route for travellers from platform to check-in areas in the terminal – the link is covered by a lightweight, tensile fabric roof. With future developments in mind, two platforms are reserved for possible Eurostar use. Although part of a huge and complex project, the Terminal 5 station is a significant architectural achievement in its own right, as befits a structure that will handle more passengers than any of the mainline rail terminals in central London.

Opposite Stainless steel 'pillows' reflect natural and artificial light onto the concourse floor.

Below left Arrival lift platform with glass floor.

Below right Detail of steel structure in the triple-height space rising from track level.

0   10   50m

Elevation

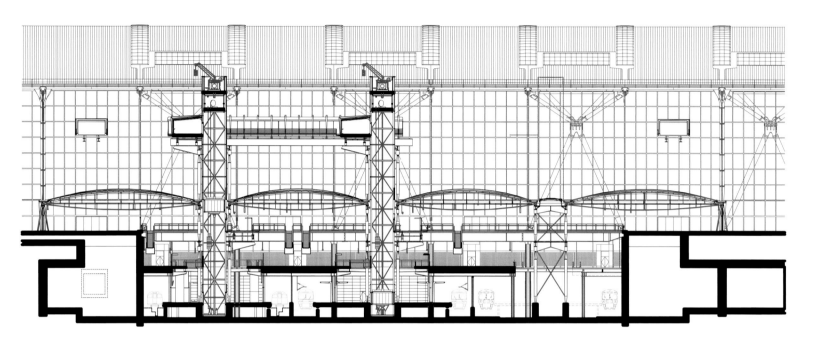

0   50   250m

Plan

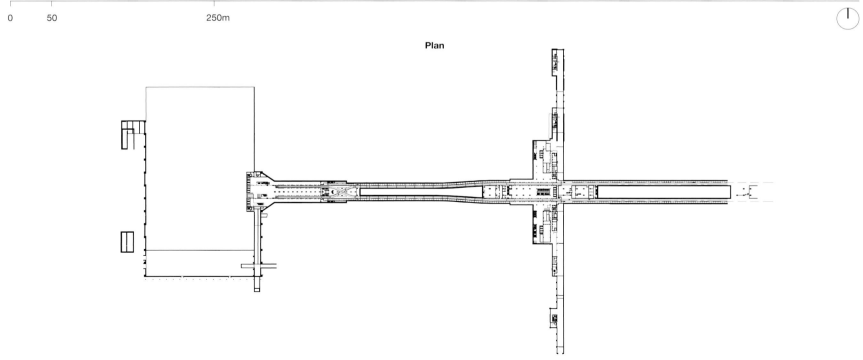

Future Projects

St Bartholomew's Hospital

HOK has been selected as the architect
by Skanska Innisfree, the consortium
appointed preferred bidder for the PFI
Scheme to redevelop St Bartholomew's
and The Royal London hospitals. HOK
are providing full medical planning,
architectural, interior and landscape
design services for the scheme – the
largest hospital redevelopment under the
Government's Private Finance Initiative
to be carried out so far in the UK. The
design will incorporate existing listed
buildings, which lie on both sites. The
project will provide comprehensive works
at both hospitals, which form a critical
part of the NHS Plan for East London.

St Bartholomew's Hospital will become
a specialist cancer and cardiac centre
with 49,400 square metres (532,800
square foot) of new accommodation,
providing 343 beds. New buildings will
replace the King George V block and
Queen Mary Wing with a contemporary
design sympathetic to the existing
Georgian architecture.

The Royal London Hospital

The Royal London Hospital will become
a new district general hospital for
Tower Hamlets with specialist tertiary
care services for patients from across
London and beyond. Leading trauma
and emergency care facilities supported
by the existing Helicopter Emergency
Medical Service (HEMS) will form
part of a health campus which will
include the neighbouring Queen Mary,
University of London, St Bartholomew's
hospitals and The London School
of Medicine and Dentistry, the St
Bartholomew School of Nursing and
Midwifery and the Dental Hospital.
In addition it will provide London's
second largest paediatric service, within
a dedicated Women and Children's
unit. The development proposals are
extensive and will provide 145,000
square metres (1.5 million square foot)
of new accommodation and a total of
905 beds.

5 Churchill Place

Canary Wharf Contractors Limited has already started work on-site for the new 28,000 square metre (300,000 square foot), 12-storey building located at 5 Churchill Place, Canary Wharf. The scheme will be ready for occupation in summer 2009. The building is located on the eastern perimeter of Canary Wharf, forming the eastern gateway to the urban quarter.

HOK is the lead consultant and is providing masterplanning and landscape services for the adjacent dockside public park along with architecture and interior design for the building.

The site is a challenging, non-orthogonal shape. The design solution has been influenced by the elegant curves of Alvar Aalto's famous vase. The distinctive elevations draw inspiration from optical art so that, as the observer's vantage point moves, the character and materials of the building change. The dominant building material will appear to be glass, granite or metal, depending on the perspective view. It is a stimulating visual effect.

The northern elevation of the building has a generous amount of glass façade, maximizing the amount of natural daylight with minimal solar gain. Stainless steel edges catch light and sun reflections – desirable in this northern European location.

This is one of the last projects to be completed within the original London Docklands Development Corporation (LDDC) enterprise zone, which was given planning consent in the 1990s.

British Medical Association

The British Medical Association (BMA) is investing in updating the 'state rooms' in its headquarters building, which comprise: the Hastings Room and Members' Dining Room; the Great Hall/Library; the BMA Council Chamber; and the Prince's Room. These 'state rooms' are the most distinctive parts of BMA House and are finished to a high standard. Some rooms contain features from the original concept and design by the architect Sir Edwin Lutyens. The changes taking place are designed to increase the usefulness of the 'state rooms' for its core activity as a membership organization and to increase the attractiveness of the rooms for hire to external (non-BMA) entities.

In 2005, the BMA commissioned conservation architects HOK to develop proposals for the state rooms and to address a number of other needs in BMA House. These include providing: a covered circulation route around the ground floor of BMA House; a welcoming 'heart' space for use by staff, members and visitors; a more spacious entrance, reception and waiting area for members and visitors; a new members' lounge and Business Centre; access to the relocated library; disabled access to the garden; a redecorated Prince's Room with new heating; and additional toilets.

Following initial presentation of the design ideas to the BMA, the proposed changes have been further refined through discussions and workshops with management teams and end-user groups. The changes to BMA House will provide members, staff and visitors with new and up-to-date facilities.

Bolsover Street

HOK won the competition to design 100 residential units within a mixed-use development, together with a state-of-the-art outpatients facility for the Royal National Orthopaedic Hospital. The site is only 250 metres (820 feet) from Regents Park and the developers, Ridgeford Properties and Manhattan Loft Corporation, required an innovative design that created a unique setting for a variety of residential accommodation whilst reusing the listed RNOH Waiting Hall as office space.

The HOK proposals enhance and respond to the townscape by establishing new street frontages and creating internal landscaped courtyards and roofs that provide amenity and encourage local biodiversity. HOK is working with Bolsover Street Limited (BSL) – a joint venture between Ridgeford Properties and Manhattan Loft Corporation – on this £40 million mixed-use development in Bolsover Street, London.

When completed in 2011, the HOK scheme will provide a 2,000 square metre (21,500 square foot) medical building, boasting a state-of-the-art outpatient facility that the RNOH will occupy. The development will also include 70 high-quality private apartments, 30 affordable apartments and 300 square metres (3,200 square foott) of office space.The scheme is near Regent's Park in one of London's most sensitive urban environments.

The redevelopment will be in two phases. The first is due for completion by the end of 2009 and will include the medical facility. This will also house a patient assessment centre, ambulatory care facilities and 45 of the 100 apartments. The phasing will enable the existing Royal National Orthopaedic Hospital to remain operational whilst the new medical facility is being built on the southern half of the site.

Bow Bells

The HOK-designed Bow Bells House in the City of London is an eight-storey mixed-use building with 19,500 square metres (210,000 square foot) of office and retail space. Completed in December 2007 for client Mitsubishi Corporation, the scheme is notable for its location and its innovative triple-glazed climate wall.

The wall takes the form of a series of 'cassettes' that sit proud of the building on its north, south and west elevations. The 'cassettes' are formed of a single layer of external glazing, an internal automatic blind system – controlled by the building's BMS – and an internal double-glazed hinged door system.

The building, which is BREEAM-rated 'very good', lies in a conservation area and takes its name from Wren's famous Bow Bells church, to which it is adjacent. The sensitivity of the site, caused by the proximity of the church and the restrictions of working within the St Paul's viewing corridor, was compounded by the requirement for

contractor Bovis to allow the Museum of London Archaeological Service (MoLAS) on site to conduct digs in the basement before piles were sunk.

With retail on the basement and ground levels – access to which is gained through the HOK-designed reception – one of the key factors that appealed to tenants on the upper floors was the 'open-plan' feel to the office accommodation.

Cisco – Refurbishment of the Main Reception

Cisco Bedfont Lakes is a place where people come together to communicate, share ideas and offer solutions to clients' needs. The refurbishment of the main reception is underway – these works are essential to improve visitor experience and reflect Cisco's core principles. The reception is not just a place where you are greeted, your luggage is stored and your presence is announced – these facilities are important, but this reception will offer a glimpse into the world of Cisco.

The waiting area will have a more comfortable feel; visitors will be able to use the interactive screen to check the weather, traffic conditions or train and flight details or be entertained with a game on the Wii system. Visitors will not be restricted to the waiting area – they will be able to enjoy a coffee as they sit by the pool at the pavement café, a facility that can also be used for informal meetings. The atrium space will be utilized for promotional use by the addition of a large suspended LED 'drum' with continuous messaging and images. The latest news and information will be available on the interactive media wall at the back of the space.

Cisco – Refurbishment of the Executive Briefing Centre

The executive briefing centre is being carried out in tandem with the main reception. These works cover improvements to the waiting and circulation space, new demo areas, a 'refreshment' of the existing conference rooms, and enlargement of the TelePresence facility.

As visitors move through the circulation space a combination of graphics and electronic signage reinforce the Cisco message, while overhead programmable colour changing lights encouraging movement away from reception around the central core.

The demo areas will be brand new, developed specifically to showcase Cisco product in novel ways, and have built-in flexibility allowing them to be individually tailored to suit particular client needs. Conference rooms will be refreshed, carpets will be replaced and the rooms redecorated, all the rooms will have updated audio-visual facilities and incorporate an electronic room-booking system.

The Royal National Orthopaedic Hospital NHS Trust

The Royal National Orthopaedic Hospital NHS Trust (RNOH) provides a comprehensive range of neuro-musculoskeletal health care, ranging from the most acute spinal injury or complex bone tumour to orthopaedic medicine and specialist rehabilitation for chronic back pain sufferers. This broad range of neuro-musculoskeletal services is unique within the NHS. Twenty per cent of all UK orthopaedic surgeons receive training here. Research departments here include the Institute of Orthopaedics, the Centre for Disability Research and Innovation, the Institute of Human Performance and the Centre for Biomedical Engineering.

It occupies a 33.6 hectare (83-acre) site at Brockley Hill in Stanmore, just to the north of London and has a satellite outpatient facility at Bolsover Street in the West End. The Trust has commissioned HOK to provide a masterplan and exemplar design for the redevelopment of their Stanmore site, which lies in the Metropolitan greenbelt and which contains significant Roman archaeology. HOK's proposals include maximizing the contours of the site to produce a ground-hugging hospital and research building, a disability park open to use by community disability groups, an archaeological interpretation centre and residential development both for the trust's key workers and for sale.

The Gillette Corner Development

The Gillette Corner Development provides for the retention, extension and conversion to a 505-bedroom, hotel (with conference and health and leisure facilities) of Banister Fletcher's iconic, listed-frontage buildings of 1936 (including the distinctive, 45-metre (148-foot) high clocktower; a major landmark in west London both by day and by night); and the redevelopment of the remainder of the 4.15 hectare (one acre) site; occupied until early 2007 by Gillette as their UK manufacturing and administrative headquarters; as a new, landscaped, businesspark offering 47,000 square metres (500,000 square foot) of new, employment-led, flexible, business floor-space (designed to cater for a full range of business use, including Class B.1, (a) office, B.1 (b) research and development and B.1 (c) light-industrial uses) in a series of six separate buildings.

Securing planning permission for the proposed redevelopment of the greater part of the former Gillette site and listed building consent the proposed major works for the alteration, extension and restoration of the original Gillette building required extensive negotiation with the local planning authority (the London Borough of Hounslow Council) and the Mayor of London/GLA, and significant consultation with bodies such as English Heritage and The Twentieth Century Society, in addition to the local community.

MTV

MTV commissioned HOK to produce
a style guide. The objective was
to provide ideas for innovative and
creative workplaces that reflected the
spirit of a youthful, dynamic media
company, and incorporated the
various brands that go to make up the
MTV organization.

The objective is achieved by the mix of
styles and materials within the various
spaces. Upon arrival visitors step
into a tunnel incorporating sound and
vision. The selection of furniture and
finishes in the reception area reflects
the diversity of the MTV group's
offering. Client facing rooms have a
quiet zen-like quality, muted colours
and soft finishes such as fabric walls.

Staff meeting rooms are individually
designed, each having an unusual
finish such as corrugated
cardboard walls or imitation box
hedge. There is even a brainstorming
room where staff can write all over the
blackboard walls.

Project Credits

The work in this book is the result of a philosophy of collaboration that is fundamental to HOK London. Teamwork and co-operation are touchstones of HOK's approach to design. The practice values diversity and the creative rewards that flow from it. Listed below are the current members of the practice; some have been with HOK for nearly two decades, others are relatively new. All have contributed to the success of the design work documented in this book, as have many others who have moved on to pursue different ambitions.

HOK London Directors

Aileen Asher *Interiors Director*
Andrew Barraclough *Project Delivery Director*
James Berry *Management Director*
David King *Technical Director*
Lawrence Malcic *Design Director*
Richard Spencer *Transportation Director*

HOK London Officers

Robert Adams
Sherin Aminossehe
John Andrew
Aileen Asher
Jaco Bam
Andrew Barraclough
Nick Baylis
James Berry
Steven Blaess
Adrienne Bohan
Tony Buchanan
Ida Burrell
Omer Caparti
Andrew Childs
Miroslaw Chmura
Gordon Cobban
Christopher Colosimo
Neil Cooke
Adam Cottle
David Cutmore
Claire Dexter
Simon Douch
Paul Duggleby
Tim Eavis
Brian Fishenden
Ian Fleetwood
David Fletcher
Tim Gale
Robert Gordon
Thomas Gould
Simon Groves
Geoff Hannington
Colleen Hart
Tim Hatton
Stephen Herbert
Farhad Hosany
Jonathan Howe
Barry Hughes
David Huxham
Stefan Jakobek
Jo Jamieson
Ziad Kattan
Mark Kennedy

David King
Clare Krause
Ray Lane
Christopher Lee
Anthony Leslie
Jean Letherby
Tom Leung
Marion Lloyd
Mark Longree
Briony Lumb
Udo Maar
Lawrence Malcic
Liam Mannion
Steve McGrane
Beate Mellwig
Helen Molton
Nicola Morton
Colin Mulholland
Terry Nichols
Mark O'Brien
Mike O'Con
Femi Oresanya
Nilesh Patel
Ian Pentland
Michael Plumtree
Eric Randall
Alex Redgrave
Barry Robinson
Rajinder Rooprai
Kean Schultheis
Freni Shroff
Christina Sigliano
Richard Spencer
Robert Studd
Liz Sutton
Kiajoon Tan
Tatjana Taylor
Vance Thompson
Roy Toms
Phong Tran
Paul Velluet
Allison Wagner
Miles Walker
Andy Warner Lacey

Sinclair Webster
Carla Williams
Nick Wright
Yi Ting Yau
Chris Yoon

HOK London Staff
Trudi Agbowu
Mujib Ahsan
Niem Akhtar
Chris Ansell
Florence Balzat
Derrick Barendse
Ana Baresic
Glen Barrett
Jessamy Baxter
Alessandro Bigolin
John Bone
Stephen Bourne
Sam Bradley
Clare Brennan
Ninah Briggs
Kim Buchanan
Robert Campbell
Michael Campbell
Lisa Carter
Li-Chun Chang
Ting Na Chen
Chi-Kit Cheung
Alice Chiu
Eve Chung
Wendy Cleggett
Lisa Clifton
Claire Cohen
Francesco Cortese
Jane Costelloe
Carolina Creciente
Neshaminy Dalal
Tim De Alwis
Alberto Dominguez
James Eggleton
Jeongsu Eun
Susan Finlay
Michelle Fraser

Rony Ghadban
Kiranjit Ghattaora
Gerry Giblin
Fotis Grammatikopoulos
Christele Guibout
Christophe Guillot
Daniel Herriott
Lara Hollis
Celia Hsin
Wynne James
Anju Jutley
Brian Keating
Angus Kennedy
David Kinstrey
Cordelia Klem
Craig Knight
Ga Jen Kong
Ben Lawrence
Jek Fong Charles Lee
Ekaterina Lichtenstein
Alistair Lillystone
Ocean Liu
William Lopez Campo
Michelle Lucas
Ryan Manning
Andrea Manning
Claire McPoland
Sonia Mithan
Nilanjana Mohanram Roy
Claudia Moreira
Shashi Narayanan
Janice Nhan
Sang Hoon Oh
Mary Orchard
Hitesh Patel
Jacqueline Payne
Ant Payne
Rosana Pirovano
Mark Pritchard
John Purcell
Monica Qing
Patty Quiroz
Chris Razzell
Patryk Ruszkowski

Ieva Sidaraite
Anna Sigler
Henry Smith
Julie Spencer
Luke Stephens
Vishal Sukhi
Zafer Suzer
Janice Tam
Marco Tandoi
Helen Tannock
Jamie Taylor
Anna Tennent
Charlotte Thomsen
Natasha Troy
Jessica Uman
Amanda Vidler
Adriaan Vorster
Claire Walter
Mateusz Wawrzyniak
Emma Wharton
Ryan Wilhelm
Clair Wilkinson
Claire Williams
Helen Wylie
Lin Xia
Suhyun Yim
Minggao Yu
Ashraf Yunus
Kirstin Ziemer

Index

190

Published in 2008 by Laurence King
Publishing Ltd
361–373 City Road
London EC1V 1LR
Tel +44 20 7841 6900
Fax +44 20 7841 6910
E-mail enquiries@laurenceking.co.uk
www.laurenceking.co.uk

Copyright © 2008 Ken Powell
This book was designed and produced
by Laurence King Publishing Ltd,
London

A catalogue record for this book is
available from the British Library.

ISBN 978 1 85669 553 4

Designed by Jason Godfrey
www.godfreydesign.co.uk

Printed in Hong Kong

Opener images:
Page 2 The Darwin Centre, Phase One,
Natural History Museum, illustrates
HOK's ability to create contemporary
buildings in harmony with their
historic settings.
Pages 6–7 West India Quay Tower is the
first mixed-use tower combining hotel
and apartments to be built in the UK.
Pages 24–5 Memorial to the recipients
of the Victoria Cross and George
Medal, pillared hall in Ministry of
Defence Main Building.
Pages 180–1 The transparency and
generosity of the main entrance to
the Royal London Hospital welcomes
patients, staff and visitors, while the
colourful elevations reflect the vibrancy
of the surrounding community.

Author's Acknowledgements
The idea for this book was conceived in
conversations with Larry Malcic at the
Architectural Association and I want to
thank him for his enthusiastic support
throughout the process of research
and writing. Scarcely less fundamental
to the success of the project has been
Larry's Assistant, Amanda Vidler, a
constant source of advice and support,
who cheerfully managed the difficult
task of ensuring that people and
information were made available to me.
Amanda, Angus Kennedy and Helen
Wylie have always given all the time
and effort necessary to accurately and
handsomely document the designs
illustrated in this book. Many of the
directors and staff of the practice have
given of their time generously but I
particularly want to mention Andy
Warner-Lacey, Claire Dexter, and finally
Neil Cooke, for some memorable
visits to many of the historic buildings
with which HOK has been involved.
At Laurence King, Zoe Antoniou and
Philip Cooper have kept us on our toes
and ensured that the book provides an
admirable showcase for a remarkable
body of work.

Picture Credits
The publisher would like to thank the
following contributors for supplying the
following material for this book:

Drawings
James Newman and Leonardo Silva: all
drawings except Terminal 5, Kean Schulthesis
and Christopher Lee: 179

Photographs
David Barbour: 75 (top right), 159; James
Brittain/VIEW: 8, 125, 126/7, 128; Rob Brown/
Overbury: 151; Courtesy of Canary Wharf
Group: 16, 137 (top right); David Churchill/
arcaid.co.uk: 6/7, 131, 133, 134, 135, 138, 153,
154, 155 (top), 156 (bottom left); Niall Clutton:
11, 27, 28, 29, 30, 31, 37; Peter Cook: P18/19,
39, 42, 43, 44, 46, 47, 48, 60, 61, 62/63, 77,
78, 79, 80, 81, 82, 83, 84, 107, 108, 136/7, 137
(bottom right), 162 (bottom right), 163 (top left);
Peter Cook/VIEW: P12, 41, 45 (right), 51, 53,
54 (left), 55, 69, 70, 71, 72, 75 (top left), 87, 88,
89, 90, 92/93, 93 (bottom right), 94, 97, 99, 100,
105; Richard Davies: 143; Peter Durant/arcblue.
com: Front Cover, 2, 13, 111, 112, 113, 114/5,
116, 117, 118, 121, 122, 123; Frank Grainger:
19, 165, 166, 167; Nick Gutteridge/VIEW: 161,
162 (top left, top right, bottom left); HOK: 33,
34, 35, 132, 155 (bottom right), 163 (top right);
Holloway White Allom Ltd/Brian Cider: 103
(bottom left and right); Holloway White Allom
Ltd/Chris Honeywell: 103 (top); Keith Hunter:
20; Nicholas Kane: 156 (top, bottom right);
Richard Leeney: 56; John MacLean: 169, 170,
171; John MacLean/VIEW: 172, 173;); Christian
Richters: 21; Timothy Soar: 175, 176, 177,
178; iStockphoto/Ian Hamilton: 93 (top right);
Edmund Sumner/VIEW: 24/25, 141, 142, 144,
145, 146/7, 148, 149; Wide Eye Photographic:
57; Adam Woolfitt: 15, 59, 63, 64, 65, 66, 67,
Back Cover.

Renderings
Atkinson + Co: 183 (left), 186; Glowfrog: 184
(left); GMJ/Skanska: 180/1, 182; HOK: 183
(right), 185, 187; Miller Hare Limited/David
Walker Associates: 184 (right).